2/48

NEW NETHERLAND IN A NUTSHELL

NEW NETHERLAND IN A NUTSHELL

A Concise History of the Dutch Colony in North America

Firth Haring Fabend

New Netherland Institute, Albany, NY
2017

New Netherland Institute
P.O. Box 2536
Empire State Plaza
Albany, NY 12220-0536
www.newnetherlandinstitute.org

ISBN: 978-0-9881711-0-7
ISBN: 978-0-9881711-1-4

Library of Congress Control Number: 2012946591

New Netherland in a Nutshell:
A Concise History of the Dutch Colony in North America
by Firth Haring Fabend

Published by the New Netherland Institute
Printed in the United States of America

Designer: Ragnar Johnsen Design
Printer: Thomson-Shore
Text: Janson

Cover illustration: "Manhattan, 1660" by L. F. Tantillo.

To the Friends—
my colleagues in Dutchness whose
works have informed this work

CONTENTS

ILLUSTRATIONS

FROM THE PRESIDENT

For years, the New Netherland Institute has fielded requests from teachers, students, and other interested readers for a concise history of the former Dutch colony in North America. In response to popular interest, the NNI's trustees decided to commission a book to meet this need. The NNI is now pleased to present Firth Fabend's immensely enjoyable and readable *New Netherland in a Nutshell*.

Dr. Fabend's book draws on decades of research by historians, archaeologists, and linguists affiliated with the New Netherland Research Center under the direction of Charles Gehring and Janny Venema. By transcribing and translating the bounty of seventeenth-century Dutch colonial documents in the New York State Library and the New York State Archives, Drs. Gehring and Venema and their colleagues have helped revive the study of the important Dutch contribution to the development of modern America.

Generous support to the NNI from the Dutch government and private donors has made the publication of this delightful book possible.

Jippe Hiemstra
New Netherland Institute

The New Netherland Institute deeply
appreciates the unfailing support and generosity
of Alexandra C. and Robert G. Goelet.

Major Sponsors:
The Government of the Kingdom of the Netherlands
and in particular the Dutch Embassy in Washington and
the Dutch Consulate in New York

The Board of Trustees of the New Netherland Institute

The New York State Office of Cultural Education and especially
the New York State Library and the New York State Archives

Dr. Hendrik Muller's Vaderlandsch Fonds

Furthermore: A Program of the J. M. Kaplan Fund

FOREWORD

The title of this work conjures up an elusive aspiration, which is difficult to approach and seldom achieved: conciseness. I remember as a student in Germany coming across a "short history" of early Hungary in five volumes. Simply said, one of the most challenging tasks to ask of a historian is that she expound on a subject dear to her heart but with brevity. Few succeed. *New Netherland in a Nutshell* is an exception. Brevity, however, was not the only parameter. It also had to be written in a style accessible to young adults, be comprehensive in content, and factually correct. Firth Fabend has been able to put all of the above together without sacrificing one for the other.

The story of New Netherland is told in a highly readable fashion suitable for anyone unfamiliar with this important chapter in U.S. colonial history. From the exploration of Henry Hudson in 1609 to the final transfer of the Dutch colony to the English in 1674, the work introduces key aspects of New Netherland: the multicultural makeup of the population, the privatization of colonization, the ability to survive with meager means against overwhelming odds, and the transfer of distinctive Dutch traits, such as toleration, free trade, and social mobility, all of which persisted long after New Netherland became New York, New Jersey, Delaware, and parts of Connecticut and Pennsylvania.

New Netherland in a Nutshell will satisfy the questions: who were the Dutch, why did they come here, and what did they do once they got here? This unique episode in our history will no longer be "one of our best kept secrets" but finally available and accessible to a wide audience.

Charles Gehring, Director
New Netherland Research Center

PREFACE

To be invited to write this little book for the interested lay person was a delight for me, for I regarded it as public history as pure as it gets, an opportunity to tell the story of the Dutch colony of New Netherland between two covers containing 125 pages—my assignment.

But it posed a problem: How to distill forty or fifty years of history into a hundred pages without simplifying the story beyond recognition, and without offending historians of the period by not giving due space to their special topics? American Indians, for instance. Space limitations required that I could briefly tell the story of the Dutch and the Munsees in the lower Hudson and on Long Island, and touch upon the Mahicans and the Mohawks in the upper Hudson region, with whom the Dutch also had significant dealings, but I had to ignore important other native peoples, particularly the Oneidas, Onandagos, Cayugas, and Senecas, and those in New England, Pennsylvania, and Delaware.

Fortunately, there is a balm. Readers interested in learning more can go to the New Netherland Institute website: www.newnetherlandinstitute.org. There they will find listed not only the printed primary sources for the period, many newly published or republished by the Institute, but also citations of secondary sources—published books and articles galore on every imaginable topic having to do with the colony. Sources cited in the Endnotes of *Nutshell* will also lead readers to specific topics on which they want to know more.

The primary sources were translated and printed starting in the mid-nineteenth century by Edmund B. O'Callaghan, followed by Berthold Fernow, and then retranslated in 1910 by Arnold J. F. van Laer. Sadly, Van Laer's work was thwarted in midstream by a disastrous fire in the New York State Library in 1911, where the documents were housed. Although Van Laer was able to reconstitute much of his labor, the process languished after his retirement in 1939 until 1974, when the New Netherland Project (subsequently renamed the New Netherland Research Center) was established with the goal of translating and retranslating approximately 12,000 documents relating to the Dutch colony.

This ongoing effort, originally supported by The Holland Society of New York and the New York State Library, and then by the National Endowment for the Humanities and the Dutch government, has been directed from the start by Dr. Charles T. Gehring, now assisted by Dr. Janny Venema. The translations have spurred a new birth for Dutch Colonial studies. Thirteen volumes have so far been published, with seven waiting in the wings. These volumes, the New Netherland Institute's annual New Netherland Seminar, and the policy of The Holland Society of New York to publish the papers of the seminars in its quarterly *de Halve Maen* have meant that the long-overlooked Dutch period in American history finally began to get its due.

Serious attention from historians began at around the time of the U.S. Bicentennial in 1976. The publication that year of Alice Kenney's book *Stubborn for Liberty* was a milestone, for it addressed squarely the problem of New Netherland's neglect by historians, the result of a kind of oblivion that emphasized the English origins of our national history and culture over all others, local, state, or regional. Today, thanks to the New Netherland Research Center's published translations, full-length works on the colony abound, and shorter works continue to pour forth. I am happy to add *New Netherland in a Nutshell* to the accumulation. I believe it will serve a useful purpose in disseminating the history of the region's Dutch period to a readership perhaps short on time, but long in interest.

So, warmest thanks to the New Netherland Institute for inviting me to write *New Netherland in a Nutshell* and to those colleagues who graciously read all or parts of it along the way. The final product was greatly improved by their input. Of course, any defects that remain are my own alone. They are Willem Frijhoff, Charles T. Gehring, Marilyn Douglas, Dennis Maika, Ann Pfau, Russell Shorto, William A. Starna, Janny Venema, and anonymous Board members of the New Netherland Institute. Special thanks to Jippe Hiemstra for his patience and flexibility in guiding the project, to Len Tantillo for generously allowing the inclusion of his important and historically correct paintings, and to my dear friend David William Voorhees whose historical knowledge and editorial skill much benefited the manuscript.

Firth Haring Fabend
Montclair, NJ
May 1, 2012

NEW NETHERLAND IN A NUTSHELL

1
THE BACKGROUND

In the spring of 1626, Daniel van Crieckenbeeck, the commander of a Dutch fort on the upper Hudson River, accompanied by six soldiers, marched west out of the fort with a number of Mahican warriors to track down the Mahicans' Mohawk adversaries. Within an hour or so a waiting party of Mohawks ambushed them. Commander Van Crieckenbeeck and three of his six men were slain, as were an unknown number of Mahicans.

What were Dutchmen doing in a fort on the upper Hudson River in 1626? It all started back in 1609 when an Englishman named Henry Hudson, in the employ of the Dutch East India Company headquartered in Amsterdam, defied his orders to sail eastward to China and turned his ship, the *Halve Maen*, westward, where he hoped to find a western passage to China, known then as Cathay.

Hudson did not find Cathay, but he did find an amazing archipelago whose main watery features were what we know as Upper New York Bay and the river subsequently named after him. Munsee Indians inhabited the area. When Hudson's news of the fabulous trade possibilities with these local Indians reached Amsterdam, private Dutch traders and mariners fought to get in on the bounty. Fur was the object of their desire, which was so intense that it sometimes resulted in bloody, chaotic, and lawless encounters among themselves and with the Indians.

In 1614, the States General in The Hague imposed a semblance of order on fur-trading enterprises by chartering the New Netherland Company, authorized to make four trading expeditions over four years to the Hudson, and in 1621 its successor the Dutch West India Company.[1] Fort Nassau, a fur-trading post, was established on Castle Island in 1614, just south of present-day Albany. It was washed away in a spring flood in 1617 and was replaced in 1624 by Fort Orange on higher ground on the mainland.

Eighty Years' War

In 1567, Philip II, King of Catholic Spain and ruler of the Hapsburg Empire, was as "Lord" of the seventeen provinces of the Low Countries, aggressively attempting to retain the supremacy of the Roman Catholic Church against a rising Protestant heresy not only in the Low Countries, but in all his Empire. That year he sent his Duke of Alva, who became known as the Iron Duke for his harsh policies, to subdue the Dutch Protestants. The next year, with the Spanish Inquisition under way, the Dutch provinces revolted, and what had started with a question of religion evolved into a prime commercial rivalry and the extended

1.1 Justus Danckerts, Map of New Netherland and New England, with inset showing New Amsterdam, mid-1650s. *Bert Twaalfhoven Collection, Fordham University Library, Bronx, New York.*

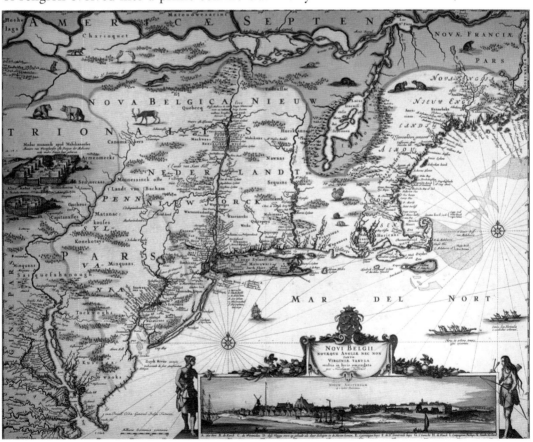

hostilities known as the Eighty Years' War. This long period of open warfare was not to end until 1648 with the Treaty of Westphalia.

When the ten southern provinces submitted to Spain in 1579, the seven northern Dutch provinces united in a mutual defense pact against Spain, called the Union of Utrecht. And when William of Orange, the rebels' leader, was outlawed in 1581, the United Provinces issued the Act of Abjuration, declaring their independence from Catholic Spain and King Philip II. Echoes of the Act of Abjuration would resound 200 years later in the American Declaration of Independence. Like George Washington, William is considered the father of his country.

Spain was weakened when in 1588 the Royal Dutch Navy and the English under Queen Elizabeth joined to defeat the mighty Spanish Armada, but not even this blow to Spain and this favorable circumstance for the United Provinces could erase the enmity and the competitive energy between the two powers. However, when the Spanish fleet was defeated again in 1607, this time by the Dutch at Gibraltar, the two in 1609 finalized their plans, already in the making, for a twelve years' truce, one of the most striking provisions of which was that Spain for the first time recognized the seven United Provinces in the north as free lands to which it had no claim.

The Dutch East India Company

The Dutch East India Company (VOC), which had formed in 1602, had by now become a formidable trading company exploiting the riches of the East and had made the United Provinces a commercial force to reckon with, especially by Spain, up to this time omnipotent in the Atlantic world. Although for some years elements in the United Provinces had wanted to form a Dutch West India Company, more wary elements advised against this, for fear of challenging and aggravating Spain, still a mighty power. Opinion was divided between hawkish and dovish factions that paralleled an on-going religious controversy in the Netherlands.

It was not until the Twelve Years' Truce came to its predetermined end in 1621 that the pro-WIC/hawkish element won this debate. That year the States General chartered the Dutch West India Company.

The Dutch West India Company

The Company's charter, modeled on that of the successful Dutch East India Company, authorized it to operate as a joint-stock monopoly trading company in the Western Hemisphere. Specifically, this meant

Africa south of the Tropic of Cancer, South America, and the Caribbean, all places where Spain and Portugal (united under the Hapsburg crown from1581 to 1640) were predominant, and New Netherland—in itself a huge area on contemporary maps extending from Nova Scotia to the Delaware River, with the hinterland undescribed and unnamed, but theoretically under Company control, too. Both the VOC and the WIC were stock companies whose shares were sold on the Amsterdam stock exchange and, in the typical Dutch manner of inclusivity, could be bought by anyone who could afford them, even servant girls.

The charter spelled out the Company's functions: It was to govern this territory, administer justice in it, treat with princes, and maintain an army and a fleet. The directors, nineteen wealthy Dutch merchants, were in effect given carte blanche to operate New Netherland and its southern sisters, Brazil, Curaçao, Surinam, Bonaire, Aruba, St. Eustatius, Puerto Rico, and St. Martin, as if they owned them, albeit from afar. "The Nineteen" employed officials to do the actual work of governing, which included privateering and even war to capture Spanish treasure fleets, the goal being to rout Spain from its colonies in South America, seizing its gold and silver in the process. In fact, the Dutch West India Company was conceived of, historians agree, as more of a "maritime war machine" than it was a trading venture.[2] When the truce expired in 1621, the Prince of Orange, Maurits, led the hawks in resuming war with Spain.

William Usselinx, on the other hand, had a very different vision. A Flemish Calvinist intellectual and businessman who had fled the southern Spanish Netherlands to the northern Dutch provinces in 1591 to escape Philip's long reach, Usselinx believed the Dutch West India Company should oversee the colonization and evangelization of the New World, not use it merely as a stage to confront and defeat Spain. Although he had in mind the southern colonies, not New Netherland, whose climate he considered too cold for settlement, he emphasized trade and agricultural development, believed the Indians could be not only reliable trading partners but also potential Christians, and he was convinced that huge numbers of Dutch would emigrate to take advantage of rosy new opportunities for personal advancement.[3]

These conflicting expectations, maritime war machine versus peaceful agricultural colony profitably trading with cooperative church-going natives, had significant repercussions, one of which was, inevitably, indecision on the part of the Nineteen as to how to proceed. Although

1.2 "The *Half Moon* at Newburgh Bay" by L. F. Tantillo. The ship *de Halve Maen* was captained by Henry Hudson when he navigated into today's New York harbor and Hudson River in 1609.

L. F. Tantillo works.

Brazil was the main prize they had in mind from the beginning, the Nineteen gave Usselinx's vision serious consideration. But in the end, a majority decided against it. Although its little goose on the Hudson might have the potential to lay a golden egg, the Portuguese colony of Brazil and Spain's other southern colonies with their sugar, cocoa, cotton, salt flats, timber, and tobacco, plus the irresistible opportunity to humiliate Spain, beckoned far more brightly than the peltry of the New Netherland forests. Besides, why should they, if not necessary, go to the expense and trouble of colonizing the difficult wilderness described by Hudson and others? The Company opted to invest its

1.3 "William the Silent, Prince of Orange" by Adriaen Thomasz Key. Considered the Father of his Country.

Rijksmuseum Amsterdam.

1.4 "The Trading House" by L. F. Tantillo, or Fort Nassau as it might have appeared c. 1617.

L. F. Tantillo works.

treasure and its energy in the southern part of its domain. This turned out to be an expensive mistake.

The WIC in Brazil

Three years into its charter, in 1624, the Dutch West India Company, with a huge fleet and 3,300 men, successfully invaded Bahia, Brazil. But a year later, Spain, now under Philip IV, retaliated with an army of 12,500, forcing the Dutch to leave Bahia. When reinforcements arrived, the Dutch invaded and took San Juan, Puerto Rico, in September 1625, only to find that they could not dislodge the Spanish forces from the fort where the Dutch besieged them.

For some years following, the Company was content to privateer. According to its earliest historian, the WIC Director Johan de Laet, up to 1637 WIC ships seized over 600 Spanish and Portuguese ships to the tune of 118 million guilders.[4] The *coup de grace* in this privateering campaign came on September 8, 1628, when Admiral Piet Heyn with thirty-one armed vessels, 2,300 sailors, and 1,000 soldiers captured the main Spanish fleet, seizing silver, gold, and pearls, silk, pelts, dyewood, and more worth 11.5 million guilders. An anguished Spain now proposed to prohibit Dutch ships from sailing to either the East or the West Indies, a proposal met with rich scorn in the feisty United Provinces.

This success emboldened the now newly flush WIC to continue to privateer, carry off prizes, and plunder at will. But Spain did not give up easily, and it fought back, in one way, by bringing the hostilities to land with mixed results for the Dutch. Several Dutch victories on land meant that now the WIC had a southern colony to govern, New Holland, and a strong, independent-minded, big-spending governor in Johan Maurits to rule it. But despite his many positive accomplishments in Dutch Brazil, Johan Maurits failed to induce emigration from the United Provinces, whose citizens were content in their homeland where unemployment was low, all faiths were tolerated (the Reformed more than all others), and folks had a definite urban mindset, preferring to work as tradesmen and artisans rather than in agriculture. Importing slaves from West Africa was the obvious answer to the need for workers. Between 1630 and 1654, it is estimated that the Dutch brought 25,000 African slaves to Brazil.

Alongside the WIC's futile efforts to colonize Brazil with Dutchmen ticked the constant pulse of war with its ever-draining effects on finances.

2
THE BEGINNINGS

In the year that the Dutch West India Company first trained its energies on Spain's southern colonies, 1624, it also made a first effort to populate New Netherland. In the spring of 1624 the vessel the *Nieu Nederlandt* with thirty families aboard arrived in the harbor earlier explored by Henry Hudson.

First Settlers: Walloons

It is an oddity of New Netherland's history that its first settlers were not Dutch but Walloons, French-speaking Calvinists from the Spanish Netherlands (today, approximately Belgium).

Starting in the 1560s, Walloon families by the thousands were driven by the Spanish Inquisition into exile, many to England, but also to Holland, where they were welcomed by the government and allowed the same rights and privileges as the Dutch themselves, eventually after a generation or two speaking Dutch and becoming culturally Dutch. Many gravitated to the wool-processing and university town of Leiden, where in 1609 the English Pilgrims were to settle for twelve years. When in 1620 the English made their plans to leave Leiden for the New World, fifty or sixty Walloon families led by Jesse de Forest proposed to James I of England that they too receive permission to settle in America, but in his Virginia Colony. They spelled out their conditions carefully, and it is worth looking at them, because they reveal a great deal about these colonists' expectations for life in the New World.[1]

The Walloons, first, wanted King James's guarantee of protection in maintaining their Reformed religion. Next, showing that they had carefully thought through the emigration process, they stated that they could themselves supply one ship and fit it out, but they required two, because they would be taking cattle with them; if the King agreed to supply a second ship, they stipulated that it should be furnished with cannon and other arms. (The fact that they had the ability to supply a ship of their own indicates that they were people of some means.) They wished to choose their own place of settlement. They wished to build a town and furnish it with a fort. They wished to elect a governor and magistrates of their own. They wished the King to grant them a territory sixteen miles in diameter for their agricultural projects. And they wished to be permitted to hunt game at will, catch fish, cut timber, and trade their produce. Of course, in return the Walloons also agreed to give all due and fealty to the King, a foregone conclusion.

James referred their application to the Virginia Company, which was not averse to the Walloons' coming, but it could not supply material help, it replied, as it was on hard times, nor could it agree to the request of the Walloons that they live together, segregated from the English; rather, they should be dispersed among the English.

The Provisional Orders

It was 1622, the Dutch West India Company had been chartered for a year, and Jesse de Forest wasted no time in brushing off the meager terms of the Virginia Company and applying to the States General for permission to settle in New Netherland. In August, the States General referred De Forest to the WIC's directors, who jumped at the chance to have this band of ambitious and civic-minded Protestants to people their territory on the Hudson. The two reached agreement on the WIC's conditions, spelled out in so-called Provisional Orders, and the Walloons signed on for six years. On March 29, 1624, the ship *Nieu Nederlandt*, under command of Captain Cornelis May, sailed to New Netherland with thirty "mostly Walloon" families aboard. By virtue of his position, Captain May is considered the first leader of New Netherland, although his tenure was as brief as could be.

As the ship prepared to leave its mooring in Texel, the Amsterdam directors read aloud the Provisional Orders outlining the rights and obligations of the Walloons and presumably all future settlers in the colony. Historian Oliver Rink has described the Provisional Orders as a "well-conceived set of compromises reached after serious bargaining," and as "one of the most neglected documents in American colonial history, comparable to the Mayflower Compact" in significance.[2]

The WIC needed a permanent population in its colony in order to justify its claims to the territory between the Connecticut and Delaware rivers, which is to say the land that lay between the English colonies of New England and Virginia and thus territory vulnerable to English claims to it. Although it was not spelled out per se, the Orders implied that the Walloons would multiply in their new home to supply the colony with a viable and permanent population to undergird the WIC's claims to New Netherland. The trouble was, England did not recognize New Netherland as a legal Dutch territory. That land was theirs!

They may have been a compromise, but the Provisional Orders departed drastically from the Walloons' original conditions, and one wonders what thoughts went through the minds of the Walloons that day as they listened to the conditions they had agreed to. The Orders bound the settlers to Company policy under a Company-appointed commander. A governing council was to be drawn from the people, but day-to-day administration of the settlement was presumably at the commander's discretion, although this was glossed over. The settlers were to get free passage, free land, livestock on reasonable terms, and a share in the profits from the fur trade.

They were also guaranteed freedom of conscience (in accordance with Article 13 of the Union of Utrecht), but freedom that followed the rules of the Synod of Dort of 1619, by which the Reformed Dutch Church would be the only public church permitted to exist. The church of the Walloons was the Reformed French Church, which was doctrinally and theologically virtually synonymous with the Reformed Dutch Church, except that the Walloons according to the Synod of Dort were permitted to use the Geneva Catechism, which was in French, instead of the Heidelberg, in Dutch. (This suggests that, although they had lived in Leiden for years and spoke Dutch, they were intent on preserving their identity and culture as French.)

The Company reserved the right to allot land, select crops to be planted, and to choose settlement sites on the basis of family size and the Company's defensive and commercial considerations. The colonists were welcome to participate in the fur trade with the Indians, but only as middlemen. The Company was the sole market for their peltry. The colonists were allowed to manufacture, although weaving was restricted in order to protect the homeland industry.

There was no mention of their request for a sixteen-mile-round agricultural zone of their own, or of their request to James I for a town and fort of their own building, or of their electing their own governor and magistrates, or of their choosing their own places of settlement. Unbeknownst to the Walloons, the Company had already decided all of these matters, especially the last.

No sooner had Captain May dropped the *Nieu Nederlandt's* anchor in the Hudson River than he dispatched the families in four different directions, with defensive and trading possibilities in mind. A few he transferred to another vessel to sail south to an island in the Delaware to be the Company's defense against an English intrusion from the sea, but also handy to trappers and Indian traders. Proceeding in the *Nieu Nederlandt* into Long Island Sound, May left a few more of the families near the mouth of the Connecticut River to defend the eastern boundary of the colony, and again to be accessible to traders and trappers. Turning south, he disembarked eight men on Nutten or Governors Island off the south tip of Manhattan with the same considerations. And finally he sailed up the Hudson, where on the site of today's Albany he left the last families to guard the colony's northern boundary, establish farms, and exploit the possibilities for trade.

The thirty Walloon families were thus separated one from another and thrown into four strange new worlds to fend for themselves, their welcoming committees only motley Dutch traders living in crude forts and huts. But at least the traders could show them to a source of potable water and teach them how to throw up some bark huts to shelter their livestock, with whom they huddled at night for warmth. At first, as they dug trenches for their sanitary needs, collected wood for their cooking fires, foraged for food, cleared fields, and sowed crops, the Walloons were probably so preoccupied with their survival needs that they could think of little else. But long before the winds of autumn blew, they must have been keenly aware that their original desire for a territory of their own, where they could live, work, and worship together in a town and under a government of their own making, had been but a vain dream.

The Company's efforts at colonization continued the following year, 1625, with the arrival of Willem Verhulst, the brief second director of the Colony. With him was Cryn Fredericksz, an engineer and surveyor who was charged with laying out a fort and a settlement at a suitable location to be decided, perhaps on the southern tip of Manhattan Island.

In April 1626, the Company sent a squadron of four ships laden with forty-five settlers (six families with complete furnishings for starting life over in their new land and a number of single men) and the livestock, tools, farm implements, trees, seeds, and vines to further agriculture, as well as items to be traded to the Indians for furs.

A fourth known crossing was made also in 1626 by the *Ruyter*, chartered by four of the Nineteen on a private basis and carrying goods to be sold to the colonists for furs. Historian Oliver Rink considers this venture to have been the "first violation of the myth of the Company monopoly and demonstrated how easy it was for well-placed shareholders to take advantage of their privileges" as directors.[3]

No one, neither the directors with private funds to deal on the side, nor the settlers, who quickly discovered that it was easier to make a living by trading illicitly in the fur trade than trying to farm uncleared land in a wilderness with no infrastructure to speak of, nor the Company's paid employees at their jobs in New Amsterdam, on the Delaware, on the Connecticut River, and in Fort Orange believed in that myth. It was becoming apparent to all, including the Nineteen, that a different idea was needed. That idea would eventually be the patroonship system, but in the meantime, if we imagine New Netherland's story as a line graph, that line would remain mostly flat until around 1640 with a slight bump in 1626.

Director Peter Minuit

In the spring of 1626, the council dismissed Willem Verhulst for his too-harsh treatment of the colonists and for irregularities in the accounts. Peter Minuit, a volunteer with the WIC, who the previous year had traveled from one end of New Netherland to the other scouring for resources for the Company to exploit, and assisting Verhulst in scouting sites for future settlements, now entered the Company's official employ. In May 1626, this enterprising man was appointed to step into the gap in the leadership as the Colony's third director.

One of Minuit's first acts, prompted by the slaughter of Van Crieckenbeeck and his men by the Mohawks near Fort Orange, was to recall the colonists from their far-flung posts, where they were living in primitive conditions, and where he feared further trouble from the Indians, and resettle them on the southern tip of Manhattan Island. Whether Minuit purchased Manhattan Island from the Indians in 1626, as the story goes, or whether Willem Verhulst had negotiated the purchase before him, is not certain. But it is sure that Minuit ordered

Company engineer Cryn Fredericksz to erect housing on Manhattan for the gathering colonists.

An artist's rendering of the little community in 1626, the Hartger's View, shows a fort, about thirty log houses, the Company's stone countinghouse, and a two-story horse mill. Two lay ministers called *kranckenbesoeckers* or comforters of the sick held church services in a loft over the mill. That year, Nicolaes van Wassenaer quoted from a letter written on November 5, 1626, by Peter Schaghen to the States General that a ship left Manhattan for Amsterdam with "7,246 Beaver skins, 178 Otter skins, 675 Otter skins, 48 Minck skins, 36 Lynx skins, 33 Mincks, 34 Muskrat skins, and considerable Oak timber and Hickory." This was the same letter in which Schaghen reported that "They have purchased the Island Manhattes from the Indians for the value of 60 guilders; 'tis 11,000 morgens [22,000 acres] in size."[4]

Who "They" were who had purchased the Island Schaghen did not specify. Nor did Van Wassenaer repeat Schaghen's statement, in the same letter, that "They had all their grain sowed by the middle of May, and reaped by the middle of August. They send thence samples of summer grain; such as wheat, rye, barley, oats, buckwheat, canary seed, beans and flax." This provides a bit of a mystery as to the year of the original settlement on Manhattan. Were "they" families living and farming on the island in 1626, before Peter Minuit arrived in the colony on May 4, 1626, or did he so rapidly relocate the families from their various outposts after May 4 that they had sowed their grain by "the middle of May"? Or had the food crops simply been sowed as a practical measure, with an eye to probable forthcoming needs? Cattle were pastured on Manhattan already in 1625 and would have required human beings to care for them, and to feed themselves.

Van Wassenaer described the busy little community in 1626: "Men work there as in Holland; one trades, upwards, southwards and northwards; another builds houses, the third farms. Each farmer has his farmstead on the land purchased by the Company, which also owns the cows; but the milk remains to the profit of the farmer; he sells it to those of the people who receive their wages for work every week. The houses of the Hollanders now stand outside the fort, but when that is completed, they will all repair within, so as to garrison it and be secure from sudden attack."[5]

The fact that the Walloons were trading upwards, southwards, and northwards is a sign that even as early as 1626 they were not farming

t' Fort nieuw Amsterdam

2.1 "New Amsterdam," c. 1626. The Hartgers View.

I. N. Phelps Stokes Collection, Miriam and Ira D. Wallach Division of Art, Prints and Photographs, The New York Public Library, Astor, Lenox and Tilden Foundations.

14

Manhatans

and improving the land as the Company expected them to, but rather trading goods with the Indians for furs, and in some cases trading food for furs, it was reported, not a wise thing to do with winter coming on again. Worse, the Indians were rejecting the trade goods stored in the Company's warehouse. They had had their fill of cooking kettles. They wanted more things, and more variety.

At around this time the secretary to the council, Isaac de Rasière, resurrected an old idea of explorer Adriaen Block's: to exploit a secondary market trading wampum, also called sewant, the polished whelk and clam shells prized by the Indians, in return for duffels, a heavy cloth from Leiden that the Indians also desired.[6]

Wampum: The Mother of the Beaver Trade

The fur trade, especially in beaver pelts, was the basis of the New Netherland economy and the *raison d'être* for the existence of the colony. And wampum, as Petrus Stuyvesant put it succinctly in 1660, was the "source and the mother" of the beaver trade. "For [trade] goods only, without wampum," he went on, "we cannot obtain beavers from the savages." The Indians valued wampum so highly that it served as their currency. They scorned the gold and silver crucial to the Europeans as so much iron to throw into the river.

The importance of wampum was clear from the beginning, odd as it seemed to the colonists that shells should be money and that the quality of the shells mattered. Dominie Johannes Megapolensis wrote in 1644 that "Their money consists of certain little bones, made of shells or cockles, which are found on the sea-beach; a hole is drilled through the middle of the little bones, and these they string upon thread, or they make of them belts as broad as a hand . . . and hang them on their necks, or around their bodies. . . . They value these little bones as highly as many Christians do gold, silver and pearls. . . ."[7]

Like Block before him, De Rasière reasoned that, if the best wampum, which was found on the shores of Long Island Sound, could be traded to Indians in the Fort Orange area, which had poor-quality wampum, the presence of good wampum up there might encourage the more northern Indians to buy it with their good northern pelts, which in turn they would trade to the WIC for resale and processing in Holland. But this plan had a drawback. It would require the Company to station several sloops in the Sound to safeguard the wampum-manufacturing process, adding to the worrying expense of maintaining

New Netherland. Oliver Rink has estimated that the costs of the colonizing efforts of 1624 and 1625 alone amounted to more than a hundred thousand florins.[8]

Viewed in combination with the military disasters in Brazil, the WIC directors were beginning to have serious second thoughts about the wisdom of colonizing their land on the Hudson, and the feeling was mutual. Most of the Walloons left in disgust when their contracts ended. Only Piet Heyn's capture of the Spanish fleet in 1628 cut the glum mood among WIC shareholders and directors in Amsterdam, where heated discussions were taking place over what to do with New Netherland.

First Views of the Indians

That same year, Johannes Michaelius, the first ordained Reformed Dutch minister, or dominie, arrived. In a letter to a fellow minister in Amsterdam, he described what he had found upon arrival: fifty congregants, two church helpers, a council consisting of good people, but with little experience in public affairs and in need of more precise instructions from Amsterdam, and natives who were "strangers to all decency, yea, uncivil and stupid as garden poles, proficient in all wickedness and godlessness, . . . [and] as thievish and treacherous as they are tall."[9]

Dominie Megapolensis, writing in 1644 about the Mohawks, described them as "very stupid," "given to whoring," "slovenly and dirty," have a "very high opinion of themselves," are "cruel toward their enemies in time of war," are cannibalistic, murderous, and describe themselves as "very cunning devils" and indeed worship the Devil. But Megapolensis also found the Mohawks "very friendly to us," and "there are not half so many villainies or murders committed amongst them as amongst Christians."[10]

Michaelius's jaundiced view of the Indians may have been related to the loss of his wife on the voyage over, for he had two small daughters and no one to trust to take care of them, the Angolan slave women provided him by the Company being in his view thievish, lazy, and useless trash. He needed a few acres of land to feed himself and his children, but no horses, cows, or laborers were to be found, he wrote to his friend. "Everyone is short in these particulars and wants more." The rations he could buy at the company store were hard, stale peas and beans, barley, and fish, and all very expensive. Historian Simon

2.2 "Winter in the Valley of the Mohawk" by L. F. Tantillo.

L. F. Tantillo works.

Middleton has noted that the costs of importing food and supplies were "ten times the expense of producing them in New Netherland."[11]

Both of these letters are extremely interesting accounts, full of precious details about life in New Netherland in the earliest years, and together they encapsulate all the themes that will recur throughout the colony's history: the clash of cultures, the needs of the colonists, the character of the Indians, the parsimony of the WIC, the battle for existence, the beauty and bounty of the natural land, the struggle between good and evil.

"Freedoms and Exemptions," 1629

The West India Company was organized into five chambers, of which the Amsterdam Chamber had charge of New Netherland. The Amsterdam Chamber in turn was organized into commissions, with the New Netherland Commission having oversight of the colony. Within the New Netherland Commission a nascent struggle had been going on almost since the formation of the Company over the Company's New Netherland policy between two factions that historians have characterized as the Trade faction and the Colonization faction.

Briefly, the Trade faction wanted to abandon the expensive effort to populate New Netherland with colonists, instead concentrating on the fur trade by staffing and supplying a series of trading posts from Holland. By eliminating colonists, who were coming to be viewed as not only an expensive nuisance, but who traded with Indians in violation of Company rules, to the detriment of the Company's profits, the Trade faction argued that its plan could reduce costs and control fur prices, which colonists tended to drive up in a more-demand, less-supply, higher-prices syndrome. The drawback was that this policy sacrificed to trade the concern to populate the colony in order to secure its viability with regard to the English colonies to the north and south of it.

On the other side, the Colonization faction, of which Kiliaen van Rensselaer, rich Amsterdam jewel merchant, was a prominent member, wanted the Company to allow certain affluent investors like himself to participate in settlement as "patroons," the owners of huge grants of land on the colony's rivers, with the give-back that they undertake the costs of colonization themselves. Other members of the Colonization faction advised opening the fur trade to all, to entice people to emigrate, for the agricultural development of the colony on a grand scale would require many hands.

In 1628 the two factions reached a compromise in a plan called the "Freedoms and Exemptions" (also called the "Privileges and Exemptions") that approved the use of private capital to colonize New Netherland. In effect, the plan opened the colony to private investors, "patroons," who at their own expense would underwrite the colonization of their patroonships with farmers and necessary tradesmen and artisans to support the agricultural development of the land, while the Company retained its monopoly on the fur trade. For this latter reason, the plan did not appeal.

When Piet Heyn's capture of the Spanish fleet swelled the WIC's coffers in 1628, temporarily easing its financial problems, Kiliaen van Rensselaer and others prevailed on the New Netherland Commission to reconsider the "Freedoms and Exemptions," and on June 17, 1629, a revised version was made public. This one stuck, although of the five patroonships that were formed only Van Rensselaer's ultimately met with any success.

In accord with the thirty-one terms of the "Freedoms and

Exemptions" of 1629, the patroons were permitted to buy land from the Indians and to hold this land and all its mines and rivers and the rights thereof as a "perpetual fief," with rights of jurisdiction and administration over it and its inhabitants.[12] (The Nineteen reserved Manhattan Island for themselves.) In 1630, Van Rensselaer acquired a huge tract of land along both the east and west shores of the Hudson River in today's Albany and Rensselaer counties. This would become the patroonship of Rensselaerswijck, eventually to reach a million acres.

Under the terms of his contract with the Company, within four years the patroon was obliged to populate the land with fifty colonists over the age of fifteen. He could have his colonists and their goods transported by the WIC for a fee, or he could transport them in his own vessels. The colonists were exempt from taxes for ten years.

Neither Van Rensselaer nor his colonists was permitted to participate in the fur trade, on which the WIC maintained its monopoly, with one exception. The patroon was allowed to trade in pelts in places where the Company did not have a trading post provided he pay a one-guilder fee per skin. This was not such an important constriction as it might seem, because Van Rensselaer envisioned benefiting from his New Netherland real estate not only by trading in peltry, but also by turning his land into a breadbasket to export grains to the Caribbean and Brazil in return for slaves, sugar, and tobacco, and to supply grains to Holland, rather than its having to continue to procure them in the Baltic. The ability to participate in the fur trade was perhaps much more important to the settlers he hoped to attract than to himself, but with few exceptions, he did not extend the privilege he had received from the Company of trading in furs in those places where the Company did not have trading posts. This was a mistake.

The patroon was allowed to appoint magistrates in his patroonship as well as a *schout*, a kind of sheriff/prosecuting attorney, who along with other officials was in charge of the daily management of the undertaking. Kiliaen van Rensselaer never visited his huge patroonship. When he died in 1643, he continued to leave it to the oversight of paid officials, until 1651 when his sons took over. Nevertheless, his correspondence reveals his deep and abiding interest in the undertaking—and in its most minute aspects.[13]

Bastiaen Janszen Crol, Kranckenbesoecker
An obscure and until recently a rather mysterious figure, Bastiaen Crol

was a caffa worker in Amsterdam, a craftsman who dealt with a damasked cloth of silk, cotton, and wool. A man of firm religious convictions, in 1623 Crol applied to the Amsterdam consistory for a position of *kranckenbesoecker*, or comforter of the sick, passed a written exam, signed his contract with an X (signifying to some future historians that he was illiterate), and in March 1624 on the *Nieu Nederlandt* carrying the Walloons to New Netherland met the members of his congregation.

Seven months later he was back in Amsterdam to advise the consistory that an ordained minister was needed in the colony, for babies were being born and required baptism. Although it was irregular for a comforter of the sick to be allowed to administer the sacraments—they were only to read the Creed and the Commandments, passages from Scripture, and perhaps a set sermon without elaborating on it or changing it in any way—the authorities gave permission in Crol's case for him to baptize, as there were not enough families to warrant a minister. He may thus be regarded as the person to whom the honor of "founder" of the Dutch Reformed Church in North America is due, in the opinion of historian Willem Frijhoff, whose research has uncovered much information about him.[14]

When Crol's three-year contract was up, he was appointed commissioner of Fort Orange, his administrative skills recommending him for this post. Adept at both his religious duties and his relations with the Mohawks around Fort Orange, it was Crol who negotiated the purchase of the land that formed the nucleus of the patroonship of Rensselaerswijck. Patroon Kiliaen van Rensselaer was so impressed with his character and work habits that he suggested him to the WIC as a replacement for Director Peter Minuit in 1632, a position Crol held for one year.

Recently, Willem Frijhoff discovered Crol's authorship of a 1623 pamphlet, "Comfort for the Godly," that testifies to his strong faith and Reformed theology—and his anti-Catholicism—and dispenses with the idea that he was illiterate. His "role as New Netherland's first church servant deserves a more prominent place in the history of that colony" than he has heretofore enjoyed, according to his chronicler.

Director Wouter van Twiller

In 1633, Wouter van Twiller, a nephew of Kiliaen van Rensselaer, succeeded Bastiaen Janszen Crol as director. For centuries, commentators on Van Twiller's administration have concluded that he was an incompetent drunkard not suited to the demands of the office, which is why he was recalled after five years. Washington Irving in his "history" of New York added to Van Twiller's negative image by making him a figure of fun with his jesting (and rhyming) epithet Wouter the Doubter. Recently, historian Jaap Jacobs has made an effort at rehabilitating Van Twiller, whose negative reputation may have originated in material published about him years after he had left the colony by Captain David Pietersz de Vries, who, Jacobs suggests, was envious of Van Twiller, as he had wanted to be director himself.[15]

Van Twiller is mainly remembered for attaining unfair advantage as the nephew of Van Rensselaer and for his penchant for alcohol, planting tobacco, and buying islands. But nepotism was natural in seventeenth-century Holland, as Jacobs points out, and most merchant families such as his preferred to employ family members rather than strangers. Among this elite, intermarriage with related families was the norm. As for islands, it is true that Van Twiller seems to have had a special fondness for them. He owned Roosevelt, Wards, Randalls, and Governors Island, land on Long Island and land on Manhattan Island, where he grew tobacco. And it may have been that he helped friends and neighbors from Gelderland to acquire land also, some under somewhat irregular circumstances. In addition to his own plantation on Manhattan Island (No. 10 on the Manatus Map), his council member Jacobus van Curler (No. 17), Wolfert Gerritsz van Couwenhoven (No. 36), and Cosyn Gerritsen van Putten (*Bouwerie* No. 41), all from Gelderland, all received grants for sizable acreage, Cosyn on Manhattan, although Manhattan land was supposed to be reserved for WIC officers, which he was not. And Jacobs also agrees that Wouter drank too much, but he points out that everyone did, even the ministers of the Reformed Dutch Church. "Life at a colonial outpost was very lonely at times and drinking was a convenient temporary escape."

But the charges of incompetence do not seem borne out, at least in a letter dated August 28, 1635, discovered by Jacobs in the West India Company archives in The Hague. In this letter, Van Twiller indignantly explains and elucidates on a number of incidents concerning English interlopers in both Connecticut and on the Delaware and reports in a serious and thorough manner on various internal affairs in New Amsterdam. Further, no charges by the authorities were ever brought against him for incompetency, although "historians have been able to do so with impunity. History is cruel," Jacobs concludes.

3

THE KIEFT YEARS, 1638 -1647

Willem Kieft became director after Van Twiller's recall. Kieft arrived in March 1638. He was only thirty-five years old, his main claim to fame being the elite, wealthy Amsterdam merchant family background from which he came.[1]

Kieft found New Amsterdam in a ruinous state. The fort was so dilapidated that people could wander in and out of it on all sides, all the cannon were off their carriages, five of the Company's farms or *bouweries* were vacant, the Company's animals were nowhere to be found, virtually all of its ships were "unserviceable," and the buildings within the fort were in sad repair, including the Director's house, five stone houses, the lodge, and the blacksmith's shop.[2] The barn that served as a church just outside the fort was also in disrepair. Kieft had his work cut out for him.

Recurring Themes

In the short but fateful nine years of Willem Kieft's directorship of New Netherland, social, political, and economic themes are evident that were to recur resoundingly throughout the history of the colony—and in later American history. Free trade, capitalism, entrepreneurism, city planning, imperialism, expansionism, and war, always war, are some of them. Also, there are more than glimmers in the Kieft years of the decimation of the Indians and their cultures in the nineteenth century. And in Kieft's offer of "half-freedom" to some of the enslaved Africans in the colony in 1643 there is a foreshadowing of the Emancipation Proclamation. There are hints, too, of the first fragile roots of representative government. As New England had its town meetings and Virginia its House of Burgesses, New

Netherland had advisory boards to the Director such as the Twelve Men, the Eight Men, and the Nine Men.

Hopes for a New Start

When Willem Kieft arrived in March 1638 to take up the office of Director, the population of New Netherland numbered in the low hundreds. Progress had been painfully slow, but now the imagined line graph of New Netherland's history was poised to rise in response to new developments in Brazil and new incentives to emigration.

That year much of Brazil was under the control of the Dutch West India Company, as was Elmina, on the Guinea coast. As one historian put it, "A great Dutch empire on the equatorial Atlantic seemed, therefore, on the verge of realization, and though it was perhaps unrealistic to expect New Netherland grain, timber, or fish to compete in Europe with the Baltic lands or the North Sea, it was by no means unlikely that New Netherland exports could compete successfully in Brazil or West Africa."[3]

Another factor in encouraging settlement was Kieft's land policy. One of his first actions in office was to issue an ordinance, in response to a petition by certain freemen, patenting to them lands they were already cultivating. This formal recognition of their ownership, as well as the stipulation that they would not be responsible for "tenths" for ten years (a yearly payment of one-tenth of their crops to the Company), had the effect of materially increasing the number of land grants or patents issued to responsible farmers, as well as tradesmen and artisans.[4]

And a third factor: Soon after Kieft issued the ordinance patenting the freemen's land to them, the Company in 1639 finally threw open the fur trade to all, in the hope that this would stimulate emigration and relieve the Company of the burden of provisioning the colony and defending the fur trade. In their long contest, the Colonization faction had won out over the Trade faction in the Amsterdam Chamber of the WIC in the mutual understanding that an underpopulated territory was too tempting for English hands to resist. The Company realized that it must give up its monopoly in order to encourage emigration and thus reinforce its claims to the land openly coveted by its neighbors to the north and south.

The Fur Trade, Revived

As archaeologist James Bradley has noted, with free trade in effect, "few controls remained in place and trading quickly returned to the free-for-all it had been prior to the establishment of the WIC."[5] With the fur trade at last open to all, canny Amsterdam merchants now sprang into action. Patroon Kiliaen van Rensselaer was one, and from afar in Amsterdam he relied on Arent van Curler, his bookkeeper and agent on the patroonship and also his first cousin once removed, to expand trade with the Indians around Fort Orange on the upper Hudson, wherein was the Company's trading house and storage center.

The patroon's financial resources, his positive response to the Indians' desire for more and varied merchandise of high quality, and Arent van Curler's good rapport with the Mohawks and the Mahicans combined to convince Arent to relocate the center of the trade from Fort Orange to the patroon's farm four miles north of the fort, in order to foil the private traders around the fort who were operating in flagrant disregard of regulations. Here he built what became in the 1640s the best farm in the upriver territory at a time when the population there was rapidly increasing in response to the new conditions of free trade. Later, he went on to found the future Schenectady.

The Manatus Map

Downriver, population was growing also. The Manatus Map, dated 1639, shows forty-five *bouweries* or farms on Manhattan Island, New Jersey, Staten Island, and on Long Island that year, a number that was destined to grow now that freemen had had their lands formally patented and trading in furs had become legal. The map is a priceless source of information about New Amsterdam and surroundings as they appeared one year into Kieft's tenure. Farms that had previously been abandoned were now reoccupied, and new buildings were under construction. The hinterland was being settled by independent individuals hoping to trade with the Indians on the outskirts of the main settlement, where the fort was the normal trading post. Things were looking up. The imagined line graph was rising hopefully.

On the map, which has a key in the lower-right-hand corner, letters A to F indicate Fort Amsterdam, a corn mill, two sawmills, Hog Island (now Welfare Island), and "The Quarter of the Blacks, the Company's slaves." Also shown are, number 1, the West India Company's *bouwerie* or farm, "with an excellent house," the residence of the Director, situated between Avenue A and First Avenue today, between 15th and 16th Streets. Numbers 2 to 6 on the map are "five run-down *bouweries*" belonging to the WIC. The rest of the numbers,

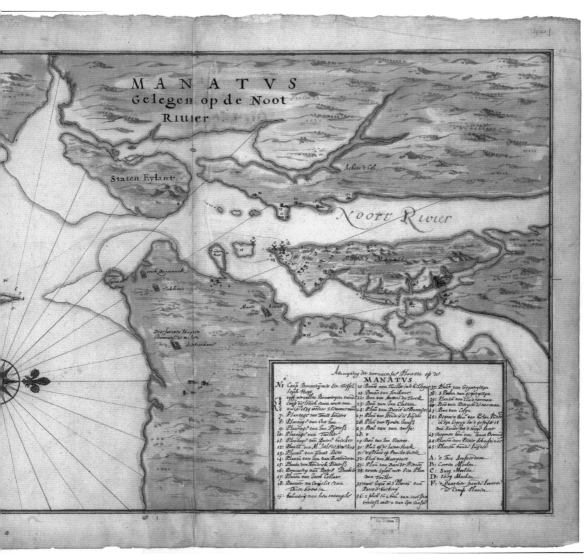

3.1 The Manatus Map,
1639. The original is lost. This
is from an eighteenth-century
copy in the Library of
Congress.

Library of Congress.

7 to 45, identify individual *bouweries* or farms owned or leased by the community's residents. (For future reference, note that *bouwerie* 18 on the East River opposite Ward's Island was leased to one Claes Cornelissen Swits.)[6]

One such *bouwerie* "near Fort Amsterdam," number 22 on the map, is described in an agreement between Anthony Jansen, known as the Turk, probably because he came from Fez in Morocco and had a Moroccan mother, and Barent Dircksen, baker. The sale included Jansen's "land as it is sowed and fenced, the house and barn, together with all that is fastened by earth and nail, except the [73] cherry trees, [40] peach and . . . [12 apple] trees, [26 Sage plants and 15 Vines] standing on said land, which trees Anthony reserves for himself and will remove at a more seasonable time, one Stallion of two years, one ditto of one year, 1 wagon, plough, and one harrow with wooden teeth."[7]

This description reveals this farmer as law abiding (his land is fenced), industrious (he has been busy building and planting), profit minded (he has planted enough trees so that he will have excess fruit to sell from his orchards), and horticulturally knowledgeable (he will wait until the right time to transplant his trees), just the sort of citizen the Company wanted to attract to farm and develop its colony. (The Turk soon reappeared with his wife, Grietje Reyniers, in another not so good-citizen a context. Grietje had been a prostitute in Amsterdam before marrying Anthony, and in New Amsterdam she was accused, among other scandals, of exposing her bare bottom to a group of sailors and telling them to blow on it. The couple and their children were banished to Long Island in August 1639 because of her bad behavior and his irascibility, but Director Kieft granted them 200 acres of land in Gravesend to earn their living on, so they must have had some saving graces.)

And settlers like Anthony (the good Anthony) *were* attracted. A glance at the records of sales and rentals or leases of land in lower Manhattan and Long Island and Staten Island in these early years of Kieft's administration indicates that the market in real estate was moving along at a dizzying pace, and houses and barns and outbuildings were appearing regularly. Sibout Claessen, a master carpenter from Hoorn, leased the Company's sawmill on Governors Island in 1639 and was paying for it with an annual supply of 500 oak and pine planks. It was a major undertaking. The lease included twenty saws, forty clamps, two jackscrews, ten log irons, sledges, log ropes, log hooks, files, cranes, and a boat hook. Smiths, masons, carpenters, tailors, tobacco plantations, breweries, taverns, laden ships in the harbor, an annual cattle fair, and a "fair for Hogs" are signs that New Amsterdam was beginning to perk up.

A Jesuit missionary, Father Isaac Jogues, who had fled to New Amsterdam five years into Kieft's regime, after escaping from his Indian torturers, recorded in 1646 of the little community that "there may well be four or five hundred men of different sects and nations." In fact, Kieft had told the priest that eighteen different languages (some of which were probably German dialects not understood by Kieft) were spoken in the settlement. By 1646, then, not only had the population doubled in the Kieft years, but New Amsterdam, like Old Amsterdam, and like New York City to come, was evolving into a rich melting pot of many diverse ethnicities and religions. The line graph is creeping slowly but surely upward.[8]

But simultaneously the scene was being set for another outcome far less palatable than one characterized by agricultural and economic development. Before going there, we need to look at some of Kieft's other problems.

Delightsome Cittie

In 1647, the last year of Kieft's administration, an account of Manhattan described it as the place of the Dutch government "in the midwaye betwixt Boston in New England and Virginia" with a considerable fort, well furnished with cannon. "Since the Yeare 1647 they have much emproved their buildings aboaut it, that it is now Called the fort & Cittie of New Amsterdam, although in the years 1641, & 1642, there was not six houses of free Burgers in it." The writer concludes that "New Amsterdam is very delightsome & conveniant . . . especiallie for trade, having two maine streames or rivers by, with an excellent harbor."[9]

The observer of these details was an Englishman, and by 1647 Kieft and the inhabitants of the "delightsome cittie" were all too well aware of the English liking for New Amsterdam. Indeed, this was nothing new. As early as 1635, Wouter van Twiller had written to the Amsterdam Chamber warning of English designs on New Netherland: "Accordingly, they do not recognize us but [try] with the most sinister means to take the land from us . . . [and] unless Your Honors prevent it by sending free men to stop their further encroachments, they will not hesitate to possess themselves of the lands around the Manhattas."[10]

Plate 3.2 "Dutch Farm in New Netherland," by L. F. Tantillo.

L. F. Tantillo works.

English Incursions

The English thought it was indeed a delightful city and well situated for trade, and they had had their eye on it for some time. Complicating Kieft's life in his nine tumultuous years as Director were the many blatant attempts by the English to engross New Netherland, which they regarded as having no legal standing, into their colonies to the north and south of it, New England and Virginia,

One of the first attempts was by a group of well-off English Puritan merchants who settled in 1638 at the mouth of the Quinnipiac River. They called their town New Haven. It was definitely within the boundaries of New Netherland. One year after settlement, Captain David de Vries "Found that the English had there begun to build a town on the mainland, where there were about three hundred houses and a fine church built."[11] In 1639, all of New Netherland did not yet have a fine church, much less 300 houses.

One of this New Haven group was George Lamberton, who on a trading voyage to Virginia in 1639 found the Dutch ensconced at Fort Nassau on the South or Delaware River and the Swedes nearby at Fort Christina, where both carried on a robust trade with the Indians. The next year, Lamberton sailed again to the Delaware with the intention of buying land near the Dutch and Swedish forts so that the New Haven people could settle the area and take advantage of the fur trade, too. From a sachem who had fled to the Delaware during the 1634-1638 Pequot War with the English in the Connecticut Valley, Lamberton bought land on both sides of the river provocatively close to the Dutch and Swedish forts.

When he learned of this, Director Kieft ordered the English not to attempt to settle on their Delaware land unless they did so as subjects of the States General in The Hague. The English blithely ignored this order and proceeded to build a blockhouse. Enjoining the Swedes in their efforts, the Dutch and Swedes together burned the blockhouse, seized the intruders' arms and goods, and sent them packing back to New Haven. This episode ended satisfactorily, but it was only the beginning. Kieft was soon swatting at English interlopers as if at a horde of bloodthirsty mosquitoes.

To stymie English attempts at settling Long Island, Kieft purchased most of the island from the Canarsie Indians. Not to be deterred, English "vagabonds" from Lynn, Massachusetts, led by a Captain Daniel Howe, soon moved onto Long Island around Schouts Bay (Manhasset), cut down trees, threw up a house, and destroyed a signpost with the arms of the WIC marking Dutch territory. Kieft sent his trusted secretary on the council, Cornelis van Tienhoven, and twenty-five soldiers to rout them and destroy the house, which they did. Later in the year, however, Howe was back, this time founding the town of Southampton, and in 1642 another group from New England founded Southold on the north shore.

Around this time an Englishman with a patent from Charles I claimed land from Sandy Hook to Cape May (explored and named by Dutch Captain Cornelius May). This particular attempt at taking Dutch territory was ultimately not successful, though it was an annoyance.

And in Connecticut . . .

But more ominous things were happening to New Netherland. The English, denying any Dutch claim to it, had long since moved into Dutch territory on the Connecticut River, founding the communities of Hartford, Windsor, and Springfield. In the spring of 1640 they fell upon and beat up a number of Dutch farmers working in their fields near the trading post the House of Good Hope, and then boldly proceeded to sow their corn in the fields the Dutch had plowed.

That year the Reverend John Throckmorton led thirty-five English families to settle in present-day Westchester County, and the Reverend Francis Doughty founded Newtown in present-day Queens, Long Island. Anne Hutchinson with her party of religious dissenters famously settled in the Bronx on what came to be called the Hutchinson River, and Lady Deborah Moody and her Anabaptist following founded the town of Gravesend on Long Island, while still other English settlers founded Hempstead. These five contingents, finding Puritan New England too unyielding theologically, were counting on the well-known Article 13 in the Dutch Union of Utrecht providing for individual freedom of the conscience to give them the leeway for putting their unorthodox beliefs into practice.

Kieft finally resigned himself to the inevitable. By 1642, "having noticed the great number of English who come daily to reside here under us," and reasoning that it was the better part of valor to let them come than to try to resist them, he officially allowed the English to form these communities and others, provided the settlers took an oath of allegiance to their High Mightinesses in The Hague and in the WIC's Amsterdam Chamber and promised to protect and defend their new country and follow WIC policies. He allowed them individual freedom of conscience, as he was bound to do under the Union of Utrecht, and to appoint their own officials, something that as a liberal Protestant was easier for him to agree to than if he had been a diehard Calvinist.

If the downside was having to capitulate to English inroads, the upside for Kieft was that New Netherland was at least being populated by families bound to WIC policies that were forming a buffer ring of communities around New Amsterdam, offering protection from Indian attack. Historian Christopher Pierce has even seen in Kieft something of a forward-thinking urban planner: Like the tavern he constructed on the East River, "which did not foreclose the city by facing inward, but directed its gaze outward, in an astute gesture of inclusivity," the Manatus Map two years into Kieft's tenure with its far-flung *bouweries* and plantations shows that he had little interest in "achieving centralization," and clearly indicates for Pierce "little inclination toward the conventional structures and logical order associated with . . . European city models." In other words, it may be that Kieft was a progressive with a bold new idea of city planning in mind.[12]

New Sweden: Peter Minuit Redux

As if the repeated English intrusions into New Netherland were not enough of a nuisance, the colony of New Sweden, set up on the west bank of the Delaware River in 1638 by Peter Minuit, was to have major repercussions for New Netherland, as we shall see.

4

KIEFT'S WAR

In March 1639, just one year after his arrival in the Colony, Willem Kieft issued an ordinance providing that "every Inhabitant of New Netherland . . . is forbidden to sell any Guns, Powder or Lead to the Indians, on pain of being punished by Death." The States General had precipitated the ordinance in response to a complaint by the French Ambassador that the French in Canada were suffering greatly from the clandestine trade in arms in New Netherland, which was supplying the volatile Iroquois. That death was the punishment for this crime and also that informers were to be rewarded so handsomely indicate the gravity of the offense. In a crime story, it is a given that, if a gun is mentioned in the first chapter, it must go off before the last. This mention of guns and gunpowder alerts to the warfare ahead in New Netherland.

Storm Clouds on the Hudson

In September 1639, Kieft, reasoning (disingenuously) that the Indians were benefiting from the Company's efforts to build and rebuild forts and maintain soldiers and sailors in the defense of the Colony, decided to require the Indians to "make a friendly contribution" to the cause in maize, furs, or wampum. The Indians did not take kindly to this suggestion, and indeed it would have tragic repercussions. In fact, it later came to be thought of by contemporary commentators and by subsequent historians as the precipitating cause of the horrendous warfare that broke out in 1643.[1]

Jaap Jacobs sums up the Indians' perspective on the contribution: They felt that "they had from ancestor to ancestor lived there and it was their fatherland, it being against all law, reason and fairness that they should give such a contribution to those to whom they were not at all allied by any laws or natural reasons"—a poignant restatement of the often-noticed fact that the Indians' conception of land ownership was different from the European conception. In short, land sales, according to Indian cultures, were not looked upon "with the same finality as the Europeans" viewed them. They were valid only for so long as the sellers were satisfied with the terms. Kieft, the Indians thought, "must be a very [mean fellow] who came here to live on their land, and they had not called him here, and he now intended to force them to give their corn for free."[2] Trouble was in the making.

We hear of guns again in March 1640, when Kieft, now two years into his governorship and perhaps growing nervous as to the colonists' safety, issued an ordinance establishing a militia and requiring that all males provide themselves with a good gun and have it ready for use. The ordinance spelled out that each man was assigned to a corporal to whom he should report in time of trouble. If trouble from enemies or traitors came at night, the ordinance read, the warning was to be the rapid firing of three cannon; if by day, the men were to report immediately to their corporals. These were the earliest militia regulations on record for New Netherland, and they were soon put into effect. But not before murders had taken place.

Kieft's War, or The First Dutch-Munsee War[3]

Four months later, in July 1640, Raritan Indians attacked a WIC sloop and slaughtered livestock belonging to Captain David Pietersz de Vries on Staten Island, as well as some pigs tended by a slave.[4] Whether the pig story is true or not is unclear. The Indians, Raritans, later claimed militiamen had slaughtered the pigs. The tragic part of this story is that De Vries was one of the very few colonists who always maintained friendly relations with the Indians and was able to understand their side of an argument. But it was too late. Kieft ordered the militia under WIC secretary, fighting man, and Indian hater Cornelis van Tienhoven, fifty men strong, along with twenty sailors, to descend on the Raritans to exact reparations. The ensuing bloodbath ensured that hostilities would mount, and they did.

In June 1641, the Raritans took revenge by again attacking De Vries's plantation on Staten Island, killing four colonists and burning down his house and barns. In retaliation, Kieft offered other Indians a bounty to anyone who killed a Raritan, and double the amount for killing Raritans who had participated in the attack, in effect setting Indian against Indian.

Two months later, in August 1641, an Indian, in revenge for a a childhood attack on his uncle, murdered Claes Corneliszen Swits, an aged and defenseless wheelwright, who occupied *bouwerie* No. 18 on the Manatus Map. A shaken Kieft asked the inhabitants of New Amsterdam to send heads of families to the fort to advise him on what action to take in regard to Swits's murder.

The heads of the families selected twelve representatives from among themselves to form an advisory board known as the Twelve Men. This board has often been considered the beginnings of self-government and representative government in New Netherland. The board was in fact dominated by Kieft, and he soon dismissed its members, when he realized that the Twelve had "reforms in the provincial system, tending in the direction of popular government" in mind.[5] Specifically, it was a popular government the Twelve wanted, to be set up along the lines of local governments in some towns in the Dutch Republic (although not in the cities, where rule tended to be oligarchic). Kieft was not ready for this strike at his authority and never would be.

Nevertheless, he did heed the advice of the Twelve Men to wait to take revenge for Swits's murder until the harvest was gathered in. In January 1642, judging that the male Indians would be in the hunting grounds far away from New Amsterdam, he ordered the militia, eighty strong, to attack, and in two separate actions on two successive nights they set out on their vicious errand, but their Indian guides managed to get them lost on their way, and the forays came to naught.

A crisis mentality began to develop when hostilities broke out between the Indians at Achter Col (between the Hudson and Hackensack rivers west of present-day Jersey City) and a few Dutch settlers there over the murder of a Dutchman by a drunken Indian. The murderer was a son of the chief, and the Indians refused to give him up; instead they offered wampum to the dead man's widow. While thus accepting some blame for the incident, the Indians also pointed out that blame lay partly upon the settlers, who, against WIC policy, had "sold the young Indians brandy or wine, making them crazy, as they were unaccustomed to drink." Further, they took the opportunity to say, "they desired that no liquor should be sold to the Indians, in order to prevent all accident for the future."[6]

Ignoring this line of thinking, the settlers slaughtered some eighty Indians, setting in motion the Indians' murder of colonists and the wholesale burning of their houses and barns. Hostilities continued throughout the year 1642. "Kieft's War," also known as the First Dutch-Munsee War, lasted until 1645. As all commentators have written, it had dramatic effects

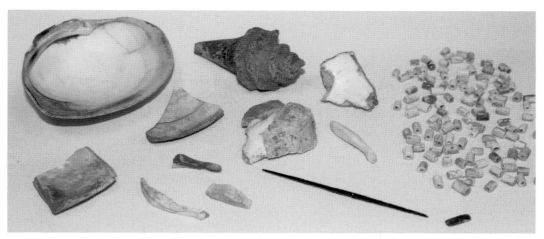

4.1 Wampum, from whole shells to wampum beads, with iron drill called a mux used to pierce the beads for stringing.

Department of Anthropology, Research and Collections, New York State Museum.

on New Netherland and on relations between the Europeans and the Indians. The Indians lost population in horrendous numbers, estimated at 1,600 dead, while the war left the Europeans shattered and frightened, bereft of loved ones, their farms, their cattle, and their hopes.

Meanwhile, in February 1643, eighty to ninety Mahicans from the Fort Orange area armed with guns descended upon the Munsee Indians in the lower Hudson, who were armed only with bows and arrows, killing at least seventeen men and taking many women and children prisoner. The survivors fled to Fort Amsterdam and begged for protection, which Kieft granted. But two weeks later, when they had returned to their villages, the Mahicans attacked again, and the Munsees fled this time in two groups, one to Pavonia (Jersey City), and another to a farm in Manhattan at Corlear's Hook on the East River.

Now it seemed to some colonists, including Kieft, that the time was ripe to establish their authority over the weakened and terrified Indians for good, even exterminating them. David de Vries argued against this with many good points: that by law the Twelve Men had to be consulted; that he himself had to give his assent as he was not only one of the Twelve, but also the first settler who had risked much to plant colonies (first Swanendael on Delaware Bay, and then Vriesendael, at today's Edgewater, NJ); that the Indians were vengeful and had murdered thirty-two men in 1630 at Swanendael; and that they had murdered four of De Vries's colonists at his third attempt at a colony on Staten Island in 1640. But to no avail. Kieft would have his way. He was determined to wipe out the Indians.[7]

On February 25, 1643, Kieft ordered the troops to attack the Indians who had sought refuge on Manhattan on the East River and killed forty of them in their sleep. Another foray attacked the Indians who had taken refuge in Pavonia, slaughtering eighty and more of them. Kieft wanted next to attack the Indian villages on Long

Island, but top Company officials, along with the Reformed minister Everardus Bogardus, protested, according to Kieft's correspondence in the National Archives of the Netherlands.[8]

The same month, the Jesuit missionary Father Jogues reported on open warfare between Indians and settlers. While he was in New Amsterdam, he wrote, the natives "killed some two score Hollanders, and burnt many houses and barns full of wheat." Shortly before he arrived, he went on, three large ships of 300 tons each had come to load wheat, but only two ships could be loaded because the "savages" had burnt a part of the grain that was to go on the third.[9] De Vries corroborated this: an open destructive war had begun, and the Indians had burnt his farm, cattle, corn, barn, tobacco-house, and all the tobacco. They did the same to as many farms as they could.

For a month it was all-out warfare. At the end of March, the Indians requested peace. Spring was the time for planting, not for murder and mayhem. On April 22 the peace was signed, but Kieft did not give enough in material recompense to the Indians, and they remained embittered. Many scholars of the Indians have described the importance of gift-giving in Indian culture, which was part of the protocol used to mitigate a cycle of revenge, but Kieft failed to appreciate the role gifts played. When the chiefs tried to explain to him that his offerings were not sufficient, he refused to listen and demanded that the Indians accept Dutch law and order. Throughout the summer and into the fall the Indians continued in sporadic raids to kill colonists, burn farms, and generally terrorize the settlers, many of whom were now of a mind to leave New Netherland forever.

In October 1643, Kieft, who by now had disbanded The Twelve and set up a new advisory board, The Eight, made a decision in consultation with The Eight to intensify efforts against the Indians. The Eight, who now comprised a number of English residents, powerfully motivated by the awful persecutions of the inhabitants at the hands of what they called the evil heathens and barbaric Indians, wrote to the States General to tell them of their plight: "[B]y fire and sword, daily men and women have been cruelly murdered in our houses and on the field, the small children in their parents' arms and before their doors clubbed to death with axes and mallets." But the situation only worsened.

In February and again in March 1644, Kieft got his wish to exterminate the Indians on Long Island, who had killed some pigs in an English village, today's Hempstead. Council member and medical doctor

Johannes La Montagne, Kieft's confidant, marched to Hempstead and killed 120 Carnarsie Indians. At the same time, Captain John Underhill, the English leader of the infamous Pequot Massacre in 1637, led fifty soldiers, armed with machete-type knives that Kieft had specially ordered, to attack another Indian village, where they murdered three, saw two drowned, and took two as prisoners to New Amsterdam. Although some historians believe that what is reported to have happened next is an exaggeration, others accept that, in the city, these two were savagely murdered, one flayed to death, while the colonists mocked the other as he attempted to perform a religious death dance, and finished him off with cruel strokes of their swords and machetes.

Not satisfied, Kieft in March appears to have recruited Captain Underhill to bring his "skills" to New Netherland. With a company of English soldiers, Underhill marched to an Indian gathering in Connecticut where they killed up to 700 Indians, including women and children, and burned their village to the ground. Willem Frijhoff has written of this carnage: "All norms of behavior were thrown overboard. The catastrophe of the war, in which both sides ruthlessly murdered and burned, revealed an even greater catastrophe: the whites also showed themselves as thoroughly uncivilized and immoral. Their cruel mockery of Indian religion suddenly made it clear how little religion they possessed themselves."[10] De Vries wrote, "Did the Duke of Alva in the Netherlands do anything more cruel?" comparing Kieft to the Iron Duke whose army brutally slaughtered thousands of Dutchmen during the reign of Philip II.

In October 1644 the Eight imparted their fears to the directors at Amsterdam: "Our fields lie fallow and waste; our dwellings and other buildings are burnt; not a handful can be planted or sown this fall on all the abandoned places. The crop, which God the Lord permitted to come forth during the past summer, remains on the field, as well as the hay, standing and rotting in divers places; whilst we poor people have not been able to obtain a single man for our defence. We are burdened with heavy families; have no means to provide necessaries any longer for our wives or children. We are seated here in the midst of thousands of Indians and barbarians, from whom it is to be experienced neither peace nor pity." The Indians, they continued, "continually rove around in parties, night and day, on the Island of Manhattans, killing our people not a thousand paces from the Fort; and things have now arrived at such a pass, that no one dare move a foot to fetch a stick of fire wood without an escort."[11]

In this same long letter, which was written and sent to the WIC directors in Amsterdam unbeknownst to Kieft, the Eight complained of Kieft's mismanagement not only of Indian relations but also of his relations with themselves. He seldom called them together, and when he did he treated their advice "with many scoffing and biting words." They begged for a new form of government in New Netherland, one in which there were more inhabitants, settled in villages, and sending their delegates to the director and his board on matters of state, "so that in future the whole state of the country cannot be placed in peril again through a single man's discretion."[12]

4.2 *Unus Americanus ex Virginia* (Munsee Indian? 1645). *Library of Congress.*

The imagined line graph of New Netherland's history had taken a sickening dive. The Eight were clamoring for relief from warfare and reform of government. Scores of colonists were making plans to return to the Netherlands. The Indians were roaring "Wouter! Wouter! Wouter!" (Wouter van Twiller, Kieft's predecessor) and demanding Kieft's departure. There was no place to go but up. A peace must be arranged, and Kieft must be replaced. Both of these things happened.

Under the Blue Canopy of Heaven

On August 30, 1645, Kieft, his council, The Eight, "the whole community," the chiefs of the Hackensacks, Tappans, and Haverstraws, and a number of Mohawk mediators with their interpreter gathered in the fort to hear the terms of the peace treaty read. With flags flying and bells ringing, the treaty was concluded "under the blue canopy of heaven," both sides agreeing to a "firm and inviolable peace . . . nevermore to break." If any dispute should arise between them, they agreed that no war would be commenced on that account, but that both sides should confer with their leaders to defuse the situation, so that they might "henceforth live together in amity." The Indians promised they would not come armed to the houses of the Christians on Manhattan, nor would the settlers go to their villages unless accompanied by an Indian who could warn them. And finally the Indians promised to take an English girl whom they held to Stamford, or to bring her to New Amsterdam where the colonists would pay them the ransom promised for her by the English. All of these promises "shall be strictly observed throughout New Netherland." Thus, peace came to the colony.[13]

At least for a while. For more warfare would soon break out and, as we will see in Chapter Eight, would deeply mar the directorship of Petrus Stuyvesant as it had Kieft's.

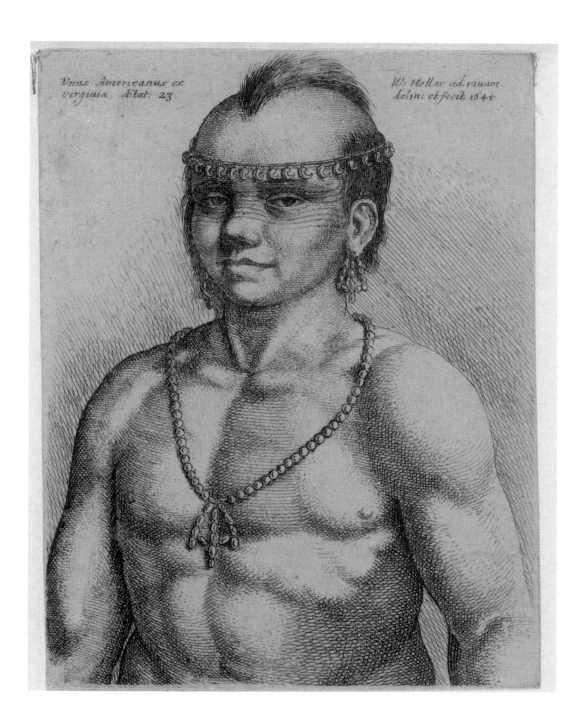

Vnus Americanus ex
virginia. Ætat: 23

W: Hollar ad viuum
delin: et fecit 1645

41

5

A FEUD:
DIRECTOR KIEFT
VS.
DOMINIE BOGARDUS

Feuding was a state of mind in New Netherland, a chronic condition. The West India Company was split into feuding colonization and trading factions. Director Peter Minuit feuded with Dominie Jonas Michaelius. Dominie Everardus Bogardus feuded with Director Wouter van Twiller. Van Twiller feuded with the prosecuting attorney Lubbert van Dincklagen. Van Dincklagen feuded with Dominie Bogardus, who excommunicated him. Dominie Bogardus feuded with Director Kieft. Petrus Stuyvesant feuded with Adriaen van der Donck and Brant van Slichtenhorst. The elites feuded over inheritances and property. And on the level of the ordinary colonists, the court records are full of feuding citizens accusing and suing each other for everything from slander to fraud to debt to assault to what have you.

A feuding mindset existed in the Netherlands before the Reformation, but it also had deep roots in the Reformation, which set Catholic against Protestant with violent effects, and in the Habsburg Empire, vainly attempting to maintain its dominance at a time when parts of it were determined to evolve away into independent entities. But then again, feuding may be innate in human nature. The Native Americans in the Hudson and Mohawk valleys and beyond were constantly fighting and murdering one another, too.

Public Policy vs. Public Morality

Whatever the roots, the mother of all feuds in New Netherland may have been the long-standing battle between Director Willem Kieft and Reformed Church minister Everardus Bogardus. In fact, this conflict is coming to be seen by some scholars as the pivot around which New

Netherland's history ultimately turned. At the bottom of it was a contest between church and state, dominie and director, for control over public morality on the one hand and public policy on the other.

The Importance of the Church

In the seventeenth century, religion was an integral part of peoples' lives to an extent hard to imagine today. In the Netherlands, and in New Netherland, church and state shared a mutual goal of developing an orderly society whose moral code was based on Biblical precepts and whose ideological source was based on a desire that all in the community adhere to one unifying religion: the Reformed religion. The relationship of church and state is the topic of Chapter Nine. Suffice it to say here that it was understood in seventeenth-century thinking that church and state worked together hand in hand toward mutually agreed-upon objectives for the order and harmony of the community. Example: WIC employee Bastiaen Crol served as *kranckenboesoecker*, or comforter of the sick, to the first families in New Amsterdam, and to demonstrate the closeness of church and state in those days, Crol, as already stated, managed Rensselaerswijck for the patroon and later served for a year as the director of New Netherland (1632-1633).

As the Dutch West India Company was the central and only governmental institution in New Netherland, so the Reformed Protestant Dutch Church was the central non-governmental institution. In the whole forty (or fifty) years that New Netherland existed, the Reformed Dutch Church was in fact the only religious institution permitted public worship, and in the Kieft years, 1638-1647, it physically existed only in the little community of New Amsterdam. In Rensselaerswijck, the congregation met in the patroon's house until 1656 when a proper church was built.

The WIC director in New Netherland was a de facto member of the consistory, just as the minister or dominie was welcome to attend the director's council meetings. But in reality, the Reformed Church was somewhat the lesser of the two partners, at least in the eyes of the governing officials. *"Nieu Amsterdam,"* an anonymous and undated copper engraving, probably from about 1653, shows in graphic form the relationship between the two institutions, as the state conceived them. The church is set within the walls of the WIC's fort, closely linked to it and protected by it, but it is also positioned below the tricolor flag of the Dutch Republic, suggesting its lesser status in relation to the state.[1]

Supersensitive about their status and their authority, dominies did not agree! They insisted on parity.

Everardus Bogardus, the dominie in New Amsterdam from 1633 to 1647, most certainly did not agree. Bogardus's biographer, Willem Frijhoff, has dwelled deeply on the feud between Kieft and Bogardus and its causes and effects, and the account that follows is a brief summary of his analysis.[2]

It began with character. Kieft felt himself above the herd. Arrogant and autocratic, he was from the Dutch ruling regent class and thus much out of place in rough-and-tumble New Amsterdam. He chose only one individual to sit on his council, Johannes La Montagne, a physician and a man of education and culture with whom he felt comfortable, but he gave himself two votes to La Montagne's one. He had a *fiscael* and a secretary, but they had no votes. Kieft's own word and wishes were law. He brooked no dissent. He thought of himself as a sort of symbolic prince, a representative of the Prince of Orange, above even his WIC employers in Amsterdam.

Although the record shows that Kieft was duly concerned with dispensing land to newcomers, with the physical laying out of the city, and with a law-abiding society undergirded by ordinances governing public behavior, he was above bothering to get to know the needs and wants of the common people, whom he looked down upon as boorish and illiterate farmers and tradesmen. Mostly, he stayed inside the fort, attending to his intellectual interests, sorting specimens, writing letters, conveying land, issuing ordinances concerning public order and illegal fur trading, and dealing with threats to the colony's boundaries.

Bogardus's character was equally autocratic, but unlike Kieft he did not come from a privileged background. He grew up in an orphanage in Woerden on the Rhine River in Holland, where at age fifteen he experienced a sickness, then two bouts of paralysis that left him temporarily deaf, mute, and blind, and finally a spiritual conversion in which an angel instructed him that his mission in life was to lead others to conversion. During his extended state of exaltation, the boy wrote down the angel's messages concerning his vocation, and he would never forget them.

The authorities, convinced of the authenticity of his experience, saw to it that Everadus, once he had recovered his senses, received a secondary-school education in Woerden and a scholarship to study for the ministry at Leiden University. He left Leiden before completing

his studies, however, and instead served for two years for the WIC as a comforter of the sick in Guinea, in what is today Ghana, West Africa. In these years in Guinea, he probably studied privately and read the necessary books to qualify him for the ministry. After his examination and ordination back in Amsterdam, he was appointed minister in New Amsterdam. Employed by the WIC and filled with the Holy Spirit that had visited him at age fifteen, he turned himself to his flock and his new duties as moral preceptor of the fledgling community.

At first Kieft and Bogardus got along. In accordance with the early modern ideas of how society should be run, they considered themselves as together constituting authority in the colony, and it would not have entered most colonists' minds to disagree: Kieft was the head of the civil government and responsible for public order, and the minister was the guardian of public morals, charged with educating the public in Reformed theology, doctrine, and ethics.

But then Kieft willfully plunged into his Indian wars, against recommendations from his council and advisors, including Reverend Bogardus. The minister was so put off by the director's brutal and unchristian behavior toward the Indians that he began to criticize him from the pulpit in cascades of accusations that ballooned into a major feud. As Willem Frijhoff has put it, "Kieft's misconduct towards the Indians was unacceptable for Bogardus. It was a breach of the moral order, which—given the symbiosis between church and fort—was also the order of the WIC. When the director failed in his function [as protector of the civic order], the minister had to step in as the protector of public order and public morals."[3] And of course for Bogardus, always filled with a high sense of his vocation, stoked by his angel's holy vision that he bring moral order and redemption to the community, nothing was more natural than to step in.

The Church in the Fort

The Reformed Church in the fort, built in 1642, which appears in the plate on page 45, was at the heart of the feud between the two men. In 1642, Bogardus was nine years into his ministry in New Amsterdam, and Kieft five years into his directorship. But until that year, there was no fine church building in the little city, such as the English had in their towns in New England. Reformed services in New Amsterdam had first been held in a room above a horse mill, then, from Van Twiller's administration until 1642, in a barnlike structure at the harbor near the fort, but outside of the fort.

When Kieft decided to build a new church inside the fort, he was acting practically, perhaps, with an eye to protecting the building and its congregation from Indian attack. But he was also making a political statement about the Company's power relative to the Church's. Note, in the illustration on page 45, how large and awkward the church appears, taking up a quarter of the fort, its 72 feet by 52 feet by 16 feet squashed inside its walls. It was clearly too big for the space. The citizenry grumbled. To them, it seemed perhaps that Kieft was saying that the congregation would have to come to the fort to attend church, rather than he having to leave the fort to enter the congregation.

Other signs of discontent with his policies were also apparent at around this time. For instance, on April 3, 1642, Kieft levied an import duty of 10 percent on all goods entering New Netherland and an export duty on goods leaving. One week later, one Abraham Planck was arrested for tearing down a placard posted on the gate of the fort. The placard may have announced the ordinance imposing those duties.[4] This seems likely, and although it is a small thing, it reveals a dissatisfaction among the people with Kieft's rule, and just at the very time that he was asking the congregation to help pay for the expensive new church. (Church members subscribed to pay, but most reneged on their promises.)

Kieft appointed himself chief churchwarden of the committee for the building project, and David de Vries his deputy, with Jochem Kuyter and Jan Damen as committee members. Kieft, as Willem Frijhoff points out, thought he was being clever in these appointments, because these three (all members of the church) had also all been members of the Twelve Men, Kieft's now-abolished advisory board that had protested to the States General about its powerlessness and Kieft's mismanagement of the colony. In Kieft's mind, overseeing the building of the church would give the men a new sense of importance and relevance. But, as it turned out, it would also give them ideas about the exercise of power within the colony, for the building of the church presented an opportunity for the congregation to assert itself against Kieft's autocratic ways, and for these men to influence the congregation's thoughts and feelings.

In appointing these three men to oversee, under his direction, the church-building project, Kieft did not realize that he was at the same time laying the foundation for an organized opposition party to his administration to form, centered in the consistory. As Willem Frijhoff writes, "The controversy over the church building was one of the first symbolic acts of resistance to Company rule. Others would soon follow—with the church and the minister predictably forming the nerve center of the opposition."[5]

It was 1642. The feud was on. It raged for five years. In 1643, Dominie Bogardus from the pulpit defended a man who had tried to assassinate Kieft, and the following year he defended a man who was accused of slandering the director. Kieft retaliated by claiming that the minister had appeared to be drunk in the pulpit, had cursed at consistory members, and in general was guilty of behavior unbecoming to a man of God. Kieft stopped going to church and urged other WIC employees to do likewise. But Bogardus preached loudly and clearly

5.2 An unidentified seventeenth-century Dutch divine, reputed to be Dominie Everardus Bogardus.

Senate House State Historic Site, New York State Office of Parks, Recreation and Historic Preservation.

against the director's gruesome Indian slaughters that threatened to destroy the colony.

Two factions had developed that detested each other. "Kieft was so deeply offended by Bogardus's frontal attack on his authority that instead of promoting the union of state and church, as his office required, he instituted a complete separation between the two."[6] The Kieft faction no longer partook of communion, then stayed away from worship altogether, and then began to make a racket outside the church during Sunday services, dancing, singing, and banging on drums to interrupt the sermon and the congregation in worship.

This was the last straw. As Willem Frijhoff has put it, "For moral reasons Bogardus no longer considered Kieft worthy of governing the colony. The corrupt, indecisive, and characterless patrician that he saw in Kieft was the opposite of the active, experienced, resolute but sensible men he chose as his friends," Cornelis van Vorst, Captain David Pietersz de Vries, and Jochem Pietersz Kuyter.

These three men, with Bogardus and Cornelis Melyn, formed the opposition to Kieft, who was recalled in 1644 (but who dallied in New Amsterdam gathering his defense until 1647). His recall came as a result of a secret petition to the States General written by Kuyter and Melyn, according to court depositions, but bearing the rhetorical style of Everardus Bogardus, according to Willem Frijhoff.[7]

When Kieft did leave in August 1647, Dominie Bogardus left with him on the same ship, the *Princess Amelia*. They were heading to the States General in The Hague to accuse each other of malfeasance and to defend themselves. Off the coast of Wales, the ship was wrecked, and both men drowned.[8]

By this time, Director General Petrus Stuyvesant was in place, and a charismatic Dutch lawyer with radical ideas about New Netherland's potential was about to join him in the breach caused by the departure of Kieft and Bogardus.

6
THE STUYVESANT YEARS, 1647-1664

The man who was described as "peacock like, with great state and pomposity" when he came ashore on May 11, 1647, would have gotten his one boot and his silver-banded wooden peg leg wet, for there was no pier to step upon. He would soon correct the deficiency.

From Military Dictator to Administrator of Public Order
To replace Kieft and restore order, hope, and progress to the colony, the Amsterdam Chamber of the WIC in May 1645 chose Petrus Stuyvesant to direct New Netherland's affairs. A military man who had lost the lower part of his right leg in an attack in 1644 on Spain's island of St. Martin, he had a reputation as a good administrator, having efficiently governed the WIC colony of Curaçao for three years, albeit as a military dictatorship.

It was two years after his appointment, recuperating in the Netherlands from his injury, until he was able to take up his post. In the duration, he married the woman who served as his nurse during the recuperation period, Judith Bayard. They sailed on Christmas Day, 1646, first to Curaçao, where he had been reappointed director, and then to Manhattan Island on the WIC-owned *Princess Amelia*, a voyage of nearly five months. When he arrived, former Director Kieft and Dominie Bogardus were still in town, and still feuding, while they waited for the same vessel to fill its hold with cargo and return to the Netherlands. This would take three months.

The feud between Kieft and Bogardus has been seen as the pivot around which the history of New Netherland turned, and as some see it the history of New York, and possibly even of America. How can this be?

Simply put, Kieft's attempts to exterminate the Indians in 1643-1645 allowed public opinion to coalesce against him and permitted the first seeds of representative government and democracy to germinate in New Netherland. The Twelve Men, the Eight Men, and under Petrus Stuyvesant the Nine Men may be thought of as the earliest forebears in New York of our modern governmental representatives (although they had their models in the Netherlands from medieval times). The Men spoke for the people.

As Willem Frijhoff put it, Kieft's war had formed the community into a cohesive interest group in which a "more bottom-up administrative style" became a realistic alternative to Kieft's top-down, regent-like government. "This laid the foundations for a political development of which the congregation [and the community] would reap the benefits under Stuyvesant."[1] About the Nine Men in particular, an earlier historian put it this way: it was inevitable that sooner or later they would become the "mouthpiece of popular discontent, which was rapidly increasing under the unprosperous condition of the province and the burdensome taxes, customs and other restrictions imposed upon its economic life."[2]

These advisory boards, by listening to the complaints and criticisms of the people, and looking with their own eyes at the conditions in the colony, came up with a vision of a new society, a new way of organizing itself. New Netherland was not just a few trading posts to be milked for the Company's profit. It was a colony. With peace with the Indians in place, the colony needed laws, structure, infrastructure, and incentives to entice more settlers to emigrate. And the settlers, present and future, needed calmness and stability to build and rebuild houses, plant fields, and take a hand in their civic affairs. As Russell Shorto has written, "The little community on Manhattan represented one of the earliest expressions of modern political impulses: an insistence by members of the community that they play a role in their own government."[3]

During Kieft's administration the progress that had been made in coaxing settlers to emigrate to the colony had dissipated in a climate of fear, many of the colonists had left, and the infrastructure of New Amsterdam either fell into disrepair or could not be funded in the first place for lack of resources. The colonists who remained wanted things to change, and Stuyvesant immediately set about changing and fixing everything in sight.

Building a Colony

He ordered the little city's first pier constructed near the weigh beam seen in Plate 5.1 ("*Nieu Amsterdam*"). He ordered streets to be laid out, ordered the fort to be repaired, the church that Kieft had started five years before to be finished, even though the funds for doing so were absent, a school built, and sheet piling erected on the shoreline to protect against the tidal action of the East River. During his long tenure he would build the protective wall that became Wall Street, the canal, lined with more sheet piling, that became Broad Street, and Broadway, leading from the tip of Manhattan, as it still does, to the upper reaches of the growing city. He was a doer and a fixer.

Stuyvesant had been fully informed in advance by the authorities in Amsterdam of the settlers'dissatisfaction with Director Kieft and with the way the WIC was running, or not running, the colony, including their wish, indeed, their demand, for greater input into the political process and more of a say in the conditions that affected their daily lives.

He stooped to their desire. In August 1647, soon after Kieft and Bogardus had departed on the *Princess*, Stuyvesant asked that the people propose eighteen names for a new advisory body, from which he and his council would choose nine. As historian Jaap Jacobs has written, the board of Nine Men differed from the previous boards of Twelve Men and Eight Men in its composition. Three of the Nine were to be merchants, three burghers and three farmers. One from each of the three groups was to meet each week with the director and his council, and succession was spelled out. Every year, on the 31st of December, six members would step down, and Stuyvesant and his council would replace them from a list of twelve names.[4]

Although this sounds fairly progressive, it was not enough, for the Nine Men were severely constricted in their activities. They were not permitted to meet without the director's permission, and they were to offer their advice to him only when asked for it, rules they soon broke. Before long the Nine stepped out of line by going about the town house to house to elicit support for a delegation to travel to the States General to protest the way the WIC and Stuyvesant were handling affairs in the colony.

Taking Notice of Adriaen van der Donck

By this time Stuyvesant had begun to take notice of a certain man on the scene, a Dutch lawyer, educated at Leiden University, named Adriaen van der Donck. Van der Donck had come to New Netherland in 1641 and spent three years in Rensselaerswijck as the patroon's sheriff and prosecuting attorney (*schout*), charged also with protecting the patroon's financial interests, which meant that he was to clamp down on slackers and smugglers and colonists behind on their rent. Instead, he seems to have spent most of his time hobnobbing with the Indians, soaking up their culture and customs, admiring the flora and fauna of present-day upstate New York, taking notes for a "description" of the lovely land he was discovering, and scouting out land for himself. Russell Shorto has written of him that he "fell in love with" New Netherland. This was not what the patroon had in mind, and he protested. But the patroon died in 1643, and Adriaen Van der Donck then took himself

6.1 Petrus Stuyvesant, c. 1661.
Collections of the New-York Historical Society, 1909.2.

to New Amsterdam, where he was familiar with and sympathetic to the colonists' grievances and where he privately began to urge them to demand the rights and privileges that were theirs in the fatherland.

Worse, he recorded their complaints about the WIC in writing, for he had a plan of action in mind. But he also lay low enough so as not to arouse the suspicions of Stuyvesant, and within a year he was named to the board of Nine Men, was chosen as its president and spokesman, and was making plans to deliver a formal remonstrance or complaint to the States General about the ineffective management of the WIC.

As one would expect, his activities soon set the scene for another feud to balloon in the cantankerous little settlement at the foot of Manhattan Island.

When Stuyvesant got wind of Van der Donck's activities, he had a fit. He searched the house where the lawyer stayed, found his lists of residents' complaints, and a draft of the document that Van der Donck was preparing. He accused him of high treason for slandering not only the director general himself but also the States General and threw him in jail. Not only the Nine Men but also members of Stuyvesant's own council objected, pointing out that under Dutch law Van der Donck should be examined by the court and released on bail.

The Earliest Glimmerings of Democracy

The chaos that ensued cannot be captured in this brief account. Suffice it to say that what happened on Manhattan Island because of Adriaen van der Donck is considered by some to mark the earliest glimmerings of democracy in action in New Netherland. They are found in a spate of legal writings, petitions, interrogatories, and arguments that flowed from New Amsterdam to the WIC in Amsterdam and to the States General at this time that are either signed by Adriaen van der Donck, or that have his literary and legal style to mark them.

First noticed by Professor Willem Frijhoff, and concurred in by Dr. Charles T. Gehring, Director of the New Netherland Research Center, these documents were not previously recognized by historians as emerging from the pen and legal mind of Van der Donck. For the full and delicious details, readers will have to consult Russell Shorto's *Island at the Center of the World*, where Adriaen van der Donck is portrayed as the "pivotal figure in the history of the colony, the man who, more than any other, and in ways that have gone unnoticed, mortared together the foundation stones of a great city. It would probably be overly dramatic to call him the unheralded father of New York City," Shorto goes on, but "at the very least he is an important figure whom history has forgotten."[5]

"New Netherland So Decayed"

The upshot was that, with two of his colleagues on the Board, Van der Donck crossed the ocean to hand-deliver his litany of the "Reasons and Causes why and how New Netherland is so Decayed" to the States General in The Hague, along with a map of New Netherland and two other documents, a petition requesting "suitable municipal government. . . [for New Netherland] somewhat resembling the laudable government of the Fatherland," and a bulky collection of "Additional Observations" to back up their charges of the Company's long-time mismanagement of the colony.[6]

The "reasons and causes" described by Van der Donck in "The Representation of New Netherland" included first and foremost "bad government . . . the true and only foundation stone of the decay and ruin" of the colony, and both the directors of the Company in the fatherland and their managers "in this country" were to blame for it, he insisted. Smuggling was rampant, taxes were high, prices were exorbitant, efforts to settle the colony were insufficient and ineffectual, and the managers of the WIC both in Amsterdam and New Amsterdam were more interested in their own profits than in the good of the precarious little settlement on the Hudson River. To put a fine point on it, their High Mightinesses in The Hague were allowing the WIC to squander its opportunities for exploiting New Netherland's potential, Van der Donck charged, and they should require that the Company divest itself of its claim to the colony, and the colony be taken under the direct control of the States General.

The "Representation," which Van der Donck arranged to be published in The Hague in pamphlet form, caused a great stir in the Netherlands, not so much because of its indictment of the Company's management, for pamphlets critical of the WIC were common in these years, but because of its first section, a remarkably lovely description of New Netherland's charms. The pamphlet seems to have acted as a spur to emigration, as Van der Donck and his cohort indeed had intended. "Formerly New Netherland was never spoken of," the WIC directors in Amsterdam wrote to Stuyvesant, "and now heaven and earth seem to be stirred up by it and every one tries to be the first in selecting the best pieces [of land] there."[7]

The States General was sufficiently impressed by Van der Donck's meticulous documentation of the Company's deficiencies to rule, in April 1650, that a municipal government be established creating the city of New Amsterdam. The following month they enacted measures to energize the settlement process, and they ordered Petrus Stuyvesant "to return home and report" on all of the accusations against his administration.

This Stuyvesant did not do. He was preoccupied with other matters, and moreover he bitterly resented the charges, for he considered himself foremostly a Company man, dedicated to the best interests of the WIC and the colonists. In fact, historians have noted that he became more sensitive and sympathetic to the colonists' needs and desires as time went on, and less so to the WIC's. By the end of his administration, accused of mismanagement, he defended himself in a remonstrance to the States General and bluntly accused the WIC of itself having defeated New Netherland with its "penny-pinching stupidity."[8]

A Charter for New Amsterdam

The supreme authority of the colony for dispensing government and justice lay in the colonial council, which consisted of the director and two councilors appointed by the WIC. The laws of the Netherlands had been codified in the Political Ordinance of April 1, 1580, and these laws governed New Netherland. No laws or ordinances could be passed in the colony without the approval of WIC directors, who extended Amsterdam city's regulations to regulations affecting life in New Amsterdam. Historian Martha Dickinson Shattuck has documented how New Netherland's court system replicated the judicial system of the Netherlands and provided all the colony's communities with continuity and stability based on accepted legal custom.[9]

Like Kieft, Stuyvesant believed his rule, with that of his council, was sufficient, and he tried to ignore the persistent demands of the people for a municipal government for New Amsterdam. The matter languished until February 1653, when Stuyvesant at last, "grudgingly," according to Shattuck, issued New Amsterdam a municipal charter entitling it to an inferior court of justice. Governed by the laws of Amsterdam and Dutch civil law, the Court of Burgomasters and Schepens consisted of two *burgemeesters* (comparable to mayors), five *schepenen* (magistrates or aldermen), and a *schout* (a combination of public prosecutor or attorney general and sheriff). The charter establishing it was the beginning of municipal government in New Amsterdam, and the City of New York today recognizes the 1653 charter as the starting point of its civic history.

The Court of Burgomasters and Schepens

Among Petrus Stuyvesant's accomplishments, extending a municipal charter and a court of justice in 1653 to New Amsterdam, the forerunner of New York City, was an important one, even though he had resisted it for years and in the end was coerced into it by forces out of his hands. Sharing power and losing control were not two of his favorite things, and giving a municipal charter to New Amsterdam portended both, so he put off the moment as long as he could.

Towns for People, People for Towns

Standards for the establishment of towns existed from medieval times in the Netherlands.[10] They had been written into the WIC's 1640 "Freedoms and Exemptions," which provided, to paraphrase, that, once settlements of private colonists had grown to a certain size, say twenty to twenty-five families, so that they might be described as villages, hamlets, or towns, then the director and his council were to oversee the installation of magistrates chosen from three names from the most qualified persons in those villages. These men would then constitute a court of justice that was to deal with conflicts and civil suits.

New Amsterdam, by this definition, was long overdue a charter and a court, for there were by the early 1650s hundreds of families settled in the area and more coming with every ship. The desire for self-government was based not on political or civil rights and privileges alone, however. There were also economic reasons: the colonists, both established and newcomers, wanted a say over their lives and working conditions, especially now that the WIC had given up its monopoly on the fur trade. By 1653, the time was more than ripe.

Adriaen van der Donck's mission in 1649 to the States General to demand that a charter setting up a government of the people be established, along the lines of the homeland's municipal governments, had positive results in that both the States General and the Amsterdam Chamber of the WIC agreed with him and notified Director General Stuyvesant to issue a charter. He took his time about obeying, but in 1653 when he did issue the charter to New Amsterdam, like Kieft before

NIEUW AMSTERDAM OFTE NUE NIEUW IORX OPT TEYLANT MAN

him, Stuyvesant became an energetic maker of towns.

Kieft had recognized that, in the absence of vigorous Dutch emigration to undergird the WIC's claim to New Netherland, the English intrusions into Long Island had to be tolerated. Thus, over the years 1642-1646, he had allowed the establishment of the present-day towns of Newtown, Hempstead, Flushing, and Gravesend, in addition to the Dutch town of Brooklyn, and within them small benches, or courts, of justice.[11]

During his tenure Stuyvesant added more towns to the number, each with its court: Beverwijck, New Amsterdam, Flatlands, Flatbush, Westchester, Jamaica, Harlem, Bushwick, Wiltwijck (Kingston), Nieuwdorp (Hurley), Bergen (Jersey City), New Utrecht, Middelburg, Amersfoort, Midwout, and Staten Island. Rensselaerswijck had its own

6.2 "New Amsterdam," watercolor by Johannes Vingboons, c. 1664, based on an anonymous drawing made in 1648, according to the research of Joep de Koning. The drawing, long unknown to historians, was discovered in 1991 in the Austrian National Library.

Nationaal Archief, Netherlands, NA-Ha NA 4. VELH 619-14.

court, as did eventually New Amstel on the Delaware. Although the bench, or court, of New Amsterdam was not a typical example of a small bench of justice in New Netherland, because the little city was becoming more important than all other settlements in the colony and thus had more complex judicial and administrative requirements, they were all to be constituted "according to the laudable customs of the city of Amsterdam."

The roles and duties of New Amsterdam's officers were spelled out in a document discovered in 1911, during the magnificent compilation of the history of the city known as *The Iconography of Manhattan Island*.[12] *Burgemeesters* were administrators of the city's business concerned mainly with economic affairs, public works, and defense. *Schepenen* or magistrates dealt with the administration of justice in civil cases involving less than a hundred guilders and in minor criminal cases. *Burgemeesters* presided over the *schepens'* meetings and could cast votes. The court was often at odds with the director general and his council as both tussled to assert their views on the city's economic, social, political, and moral development.

In economic affairs, the court supervised those whose work directly affected the populace: men whose jobs it was to measure grains and mark casks with brands, tappers and tavern keepers as to hours, measures, price, and quality of food and drink, and bakers and bolters as to the size, weight, quality, and price of bread. When a public weigh house was established in the city, the *burgemeesters* and *schepenen* supervised its operation and the fees it charged. In public works, they financed, built, and maintained roads and canals and issued rules for the collection of refuse, the erecting of fences against animals, fire-prevention measures, and the "rattle watch," which patrolled at night to maintain order and safety. Although the defense of the city and the colony was the responsibility of the Company, the *burgemeesters* and *schepenen* had to assist with financing, in return for which help they received perks—for example, a portion of the WIC's fees on wine imports. The building of the wall that became Wall Street was one of the defensive measures that required cooperation between court and council in this way.

The third office, that of *schout*, was a bit of a sore point. In 1653, when the city received its charter and the court was set up, Petrus Stuyvesant retained Cornelis van Tienhoven, Willem Kieft's controversial war-mongering, Indian-hating "evil genius," to serve as both *schout* on the court, able to prosecute in serious criminal cases, and *fiscael*, a member of the Director General's council charged to defend the rights of the WIC in, say, cases of smuggling or breaches of behavior on the part of WIC employees. This was not a satisfactory arrangement, for it combined in one official two positions of different statuses with different judicial competencies.[13] The *burgemeesters* and *schepenen* wanted the two offices to be separate, but this was not to happen until 1660, four years after Van Tienhoven had absconded from New Netherland in disgrace.

One of Stuyvesant's challenges in New Netherland was to balance the needs and wants of the people with the wishes and demands of the Dutch West India Company. The *schout/fiscael* impasse illustrates that this was not always easy. As the Court of Burgomasters and Schepens in New Amsterdam evolved over the next decade, it would broaden and deepen its responsibilities and influence, so much so that when the English took over the administration of what they renamed New York, they retained the Dutch judicial system, simply changing the names of *burgemeesters* to mayors, *schepenen* to aldermen, and *schouts* to sheriffs.

Harlem Village

A case in which Stuyvesant and council bent over backwards to answer the needs of the people at the same time as furthering the goal of the WIC to populate its territory is that of Harlem Village. A settlement at the northern end of Manhattan, Harlem Village had been laid waste in 1655 by Indians, who in bloody raids during the Second Dutch-Munsee War murdered and took captive many of its inhabitants and caused survivors to flee for their lives. In 1658, in an attempt to restart *Nieuw Haerlem*, where incidentally Stuyvesant owned land in partnership with others, Stuyvesant and council offered the colonists generous parcels of farmland as large as forty-eight acres and sixteen acres of swampland free of tenths for fifteen years.

They also promised to send twelve to fifteen soldiers at the Company's expense to protect the people from any further Indian attacks if the people would return. To encourage them, they offered other lures: They promised a court of justice and a Reformed minister, and they agreed to build a wagon road from the village to New Amsterdam, set up a ferry from the village over the Harlem River into English-occupied towns in today's Bronx and Westchester County, and organize a cattle and horse market. Historian James Riker recorded the success of this effort.[14] Soon streets were laid out, houses built, gardens and fields planted, and settlers of French, Walloon, Danish, Swedish, German, and

Dutch origins were governing themselves in a court and attending a church served by a *voorleser*, another lay office.

The Burgher Guard and Burgher Right

Another Dutch institution that made the crossing to New Netherland was the burgher guard, a sort of militia, described by Jaap Jacobs as a "community of citizens, bound in solidarity, who stood up for one another and who were collectively responsible for the maintenance of peace, order, and security."[15] Members of the burgher guard enjoyed rights, such as the right to practice certain trades or crafts (for example, baking in New Netherland), in return for which they had to pay taxes and perform military duty.

Out of the burgher guard grew the custom of the burgher right, which constituted a two-level system of municipal citizenship. It was instituted in New Amsterdam in 1657 partly as a defense against the itinerant fur traders who arrived in the trading season and made straight for Beverwijck to obtain pelts from the Indians, which they then sold at less than a resident could who had to maintain a house and pay taxes and burgher-guard fees for military protection.

There were a small burgher right and a great burgher right. The small burgher right provided anyone who had resided in New Amsterdam for a year and six weeks, or anyone who paid twenty guilders for it, the right to practice a trade or carry on business. For fifty guilders, residents, dominies, and military officers could acquire the great burgher right, which qualified them, in addition to practicing a trade and carrying on business, to hold office. Twenty residents, including Stuyvesant, purchased the great burgher right, and 237 the small burgher right.[16]

The itinerant traders were somewhat deterred by this attempt at regulating them, but not totally, for Stuyvesant was partially foiled in his efforts to protect New Amsterdam from the inflation they caused by policy decisions of his employers in Amsterdam. Historian Simon Middleton has explained the complex relationships between the WIC's free-trade policy, Stuyvesant's reform measures to protect local consumers, and the dissatisfaction of the colonists/consumers with unregulated trade, which came to a famous crisis over the shortage of bread in New Amsterdam, resulting in new regulations in regard to weight, type, and quality. [17]

Things were seldom perfect in Petrus Stuyvesant's colony.

7

THE STUYVESANT YEARS:
THE FRACTIOUS FIFTIES

Stuyvesant has always been portrayed as autocratic and tyrannical, but he was also a conscientious leader who passionately wanted New Netherland to succeed. Indeed, if Adriaen van der Donck had fallen in love with the colony, Stuyvesant was equally smitten with it, and he had myriad opportunities to prove his devotion.

One of these opportunities offered itself in 1650. In 1648, about five years after the untimely demise of the Patroon Kiliaen van Rensselaer in 1643, and one year into Petrus Stuyvesant's tenure as director general of New Netherland, Kiliaen's family appointed Brant Aertsz van Slichtenhorst to manage Rensselaerswijck as director and *schout*.

Van Slichtenhorst's instructions spelled out that as manager and director he was in charge of collecting the patroon's fees from the farmers and millers in the colony, attending to all matters pertaining to the boundaries of the colony and all of the prerogatives of the patroon, and of maintaining good relations with the Indians. As *schout*, he was the chief officer of the court at Rensselaerswijck, charged with seeing that the inhabitants obeyed the local ordinances and were punished if they did not.

Smackdown on the Hudson

Upon arrival in New Amsterdam, Van Slichtenhorst's instructions were to present himself to Petrus Stuyvesant and offer the patroon's greetings and wishes for cooperation between the two. It seems to have been beneath Van Slichtenhorst's dignity as a man of near sixty years and the director of a colony within a colony to defer to the much younger Stuyvesant, thirty-seven. In a court case in the Arnhem archives it appears that the older man got drunk and behaved "as if he came there in order to have authority over Stuyvesant and as if he wanted to rule over him."[1]

Shortly thereafter, in early May 1648, he refused an order from Stuyvesant to observe a day of fasting and thanksgiving in honor of the Peace of Westphalia, which ended the Eighty Years' War with Spain. Stuyvesant, always one to stand on ceremony, was offended, and when he got wind that Van Slichtenhorst had begun to grant lots and building permits for houses on the west side of the Hudson, around Fort Orange, he took action, ordering Van Slichtenhorst not to build anything within the area of a cannon shot of the fort.

Van Slichtenhorst retorted that the land under and around the fort belonged to the patroon, and added another provocation by ordering the colonists not to use the patroon's wagons and horses to help in the repairs to the fort from winter damage. Then he heaped insult on injury by forbidding workers in the employ of the WIC from quarrying stone and cutting wood on the patroon's lands without his express permission. His effrontery knew no bounds when he bought land from the Indians to add to the already huge patroonship and when he suggested that Stuyvesant was too cozy with the English (he had been corresponding with Governor John Winthrop, Jr., over the disputed eastern boundaries of New Netherland).

Stuyvesant could not abide these assaults on his authority, or any actions that could weaken the fort, which was central to the fur trade, to the colony's defense, and to the honor of his own office, and he ordered the new houses to be torn down. Van Slichtenhorst went on issuing building permits; Stuyvesant sent soldiers up from New Amsterdam to help in the demolition. Van Slichtenhorst pointed out that houses were built around Fort Amsterdam, so why not around Fort Orange. In October Stuyvesant ordered Van Slichtenhorst to appear before him and the council at the first court day in April 1649.

In the meantime, the population of Fort Orange or Beverwijck was growing to the point where church services were now held there, rather than on the east side of the river as before. Beverwijck was becoming, right under Stuyvesant's nose, a real community, with church, school, poor house, tavern, roads, and bridges.

Van Slichtenhorst did not deign to appear in court in New Amsterdam in April 1649 as ordered, and then he went a step too far and tore down a WIC placard concerning excise taxes. At this, Stuyvesant had him brought to New Amsterdam and thrown in jail. He promptly escaped and sailed back to the center of Rensselaerswijck.

FORT ORANGE, RENSSELAERSWIJCK
ALBANY, NEW YORK, CIRCA 1650

7.1 "Fort Orange and the Patroon's House" by L. F. Tantillo.

L. F. Tantillo works

Fed up, on March 5, 1652, the council proclaimed the WIC's jurisdiction around the fort and ordered the erection of boundary posts to mark its perimeter.

Van Slichtenhorst promptly tore down copies of the proclamation, at which point the commander of the fort apprehended him, sailed him down the river, and threw him in jail again, where he languished for sixteen months. While he was in jail, the patroon replaced him, with the blessing of the Amsterdam Chamber of the WIC, installing Kiliaen's son Jan Baptist van Rensselaer in the office. In essence, as Janny Venema has written, the WIC gave Stuyvesant a mandate to uphold the sovereignty of the fort, including the area within 3,000 feet of its perimeter.[2] That power struggle, for one, was over. Stuyvesant had defended his precious colony.

The Hartford Treaty

But another struggle loomed concerning the ever-beset boundary issues with the English colonies. As Stuyvesant sailed in the winter and

spring of 1647 to his new post as director general of the colony of New
Netherland, he was not only well aware of the fraught situation in New
Amsterdam, where the colonists were demanding rights and privileges.
He was aware, too, that his employers, the Amsterdam directors of the
WIC, were eager for him to acquire recognition of New Netherland's
territorial claims by the English in New England.

By this time, four English colonies comprised a defensive
confederation known as the United Colonies of New England: The four
were Plymouth Plantation and the Massachusetts Bay Colony and their
offshoots, New Haven and Connecticut. Connecticut colony was centered
at present-day Hartford, at the very spot where in 1624 the Dutch had
established what they came to call the House of Good Hope, their trading
post on the Fresh River, today's Connecticut River. The English had
never recognized the colony of New Netherland as a legal entity. Their
claim to all the area from Newfoundland down to Virginia was based on
fifteenth-century Doctrine of Discovery formulations and on English

common law, both of which stated that land ownership was governed by the right of first occupation. On the other hand, Roman Dutch law (also based on the Doctrine of Discovery) governed the Dutch claim to New Netherland, which held that land ownership was governed by "use and occupation."[3]

As historian Jaap Jacobs has pointed out, the occupation of said lands underlay both claims, but the English interpretation of the concept was broader than the Dutch understanding. The English simply dismissed the Dutch claim to New Netherland. As they put it, they "were the First Planters of the Northerne firme land of America, and have plantations there from the Southernmost part of Virginia . . . to Newfoundland . . . ; and not knowing of any plantation of the Netherlanders there, *save a small number up in Hudson's River*, Wee thinke it is not necessary at present to settle the limits, which may be done hereafter in convenient tyme."[4]

The problem with occupation as a governing principle was that there were as many as 30,000 English settlers occupying New England (some of whom as we've seen were making their homes in New Netherland on Long Island), whereas the Dutch in 1650 numbered a paltry 3,000 at most. How could the Dutch possibly defend their claim in the face of such an imbalance? In the end, they couldn't, but Stuyvesant made a brave try at fixing the boundaries in the so-called Treaty of Hartford in 1650, remembered as one of his accomplishments.

The terms of the treaty provided that, "upon Long Island a line run from the westernmost part of Oyster Bay, so, and in a straight and direct line, to the sea, shall be the bounds betwixt the English and Dutch there; the easterly part to belong to the English, the westernmost part to the Dutch." Since the English were already occupying the eastern end of Long Island, this was simply an acknowledgment of the status quo. The second term stated that a boundary line was to begin on the west side of Greenwich Bay and to run north for twenty miles into the colony of New Haven, with the Dutch having rights to a corridor ten miles wide east of the Hudson River, six miles wide of which were to remain unpeopled. This too was satisfactory, as the Dutch viewed the corridor as one for fur trading, not agricultural development. Stuyvesant had had to agree to English encroachments on New Netherland, but at least he had got the English to accept limits to their claim to the whole colony. The WIC directors in the Amsterdam Chamber had reason to be satisfied with their man in America.[5]

New Sweden

In 1655, exactly halfway through his seventeen-year administration (by far the longest of any director general of the colony), Stuyvesant undertook another successful defense of New Netherland's ever-contested boundaries. With a fleet of seven ships, including *De Waegh*, a large warship the WIC had chartered from the city of Amsterdam, and five companies of soldiers, he sailed from Manhattan on September 5, 1655, to oust the Swedes from their forts and their settlements on the Delaware River, which the Dutch called the Suyt, or South, River. Twenty days later, the Swedes surrendered, without a shot having been fired, and the Delaware was Dutch again.[6]

Whatever were Swedes doing with forts and settlements on the Delaware River in New Netherland anyway? After his dismissal as Director of New Netherland in 1632, Peter Minuit joined the employ of the Royal Swedish General Trading Company, which was chartered, with Dutch financial backing, by Christina, Queen of Sweden, in 1637. The Company's intention was to enter the fur trade, the Delaware area being its target, and Peter Minuit was chosen to lead the charge because of his knowledge of the local Indians and the geographical features of the area. He arrived in the valley in 1638, negotiated with the Indians for land on the site of today's Wilmington, Delaware, built a fort, which he called Fort Christina, and started trading in territory that he fully knew was a Dutch West India Company colony.

When he learned of Fort Christina's existence, Kieft fired off a protest, but Minuit ignored him. Unsure of what to do next, being as it was only his first year in New Netherland, Kieft did nothing.

Fort Christina was not far from Fort Nassau, the Dutch trading post to the north on the eastern shore of the river, today's Gloucester, New Jersey, and Kieft should have been more concerned than he was. Peter Minuit had cleverly located the Swedish fort on the west shore of the river at a spot much more convenient for the Susquahannock Indians, who had to cross the Delaware with their peltry to get to Fort Nassau, which involved retrieving hidden canoes, packing the peltry into the canoes, and paddling across the river. With Fort Christina open for business, the usefulness of the Dutch trading operation at Fort Nassau was snuffed out on the spot. And the Swedish venture became something of a double disaster for the Dutch, for Fort Christina south of Fort Nassau was also in a position to obstruct river traffic to the Dutch post. By 1643, the Swedes had built another two forts, Fort

Elfsborg on an island off the east shore, and Fort New Gotheburg on Tinicum Island in the Delaware. The Delaware was firmly in Swedish hands and defended by Swedish cannons.

7.2 "The Ferry (near Fort Orange, 1643)" by L. F. Tantillo.
L. F. Tantillo works

Instead of risking a messy confrontation, Kieft made the best of a bad hand by cooperating with the Swedes. In 1641, for instance, when the venturing English contingent from New Haven under George Lumberton sailed up the river to start their own settlement and trading post, the Swedes and Dutch joined forces to oust them and burn down their buildings.

By the time Stuyvesant came on the scene in 1647, New Sweden was a going concern with several hundred settlers, although somewhat hampered by the inconsistent supply of trade goods coming from the mother country. At one point, no ship came from Sweden for five long years. As Charles Gehring put it, "The Indians hated nothing more than to struggle through the wilderness with heavy packs of furs only to find that the European traders had nothing to offer."[7] It is estimated that these heavy packs of furs totaled between thirty and forty thousand pelts annually. Still, the Swedes, their forts, and their farms, which were manned by royal fiat by Sweden's poachers, deserters, debtors, and adulterers ("bandits," in one Dutch officer's description) were a constant thorn in the WIC's side.

Stuyvesant was convinced, however, that the English were more of a threat to New Netherland in the Delaware Valley than the Swedes: "We are of the opinion," he wrote, "that if [the English] were to go settle there [the Delaware], they would also attempt to occupy from behind this River [the Hudson] between the Colony [of Rensselaerswijck] and this place [Manhattan]. And thus divert the entire trade and separate the Colony of Rensselaerswijck from this place [Manhattan]."[8] In other words, he feared that the English, particularly the aggressive and determined New Haven people, would learn what the Dutch already knew: that one of the several origins of the Delaware River was the east branch, which originated some sixty miles southwest of Fort Orange and Rensselaerswijck (somewhere east of today's Oneonta, New York, and west of Kingston), and that whoever controlled the upper Delaware Valley would also have access to the Mohawk Indians and the fur trade operating out of Fort Orange, today's Albany, New York. It was a daunting thought.

In 1650, at Hartford, Stuyvesant was able to defuse this threat by persuading the colonies of Plymouth, Massachusetts, and Connecticut to agree that any future incursion of the New Haven people into the Delaware would be unacceptable and that no English settlement there would be defended in the case of Indian attack. With his mind at rest about this matter, he now invaded the South River, literally dismantled Fort Nassau, bought land from the Indians on the auspicious west shore of the Delaware, south of Fort Christina, and moved what he salvaged from Fort Nassau to this site, today's New Castle, Delaware. He thus deftly turned a geographical disadvantage to a commanding advantage. He called it Fort Casimir.

Two years later, in 1652, the first of several Anglo-Dutch wars broke out in Europe, and Stuyvesant's concerns reverted to the Hudson and the defense of New Amsterdam against possible attack from England or New England. Just as this war ended in 1654, and while Stuyvesant's back was still turned from the South River, the Swedes under a new governor overwhelmed Fort Casimir on May 30, 1654, Trinity Sunday. They renamed it Fort Trefaldighet, the Swedish word for trinity. Again not a shot was fired.

The directors in Amsterdam were furious and ordered Stuyvesant to do his utmost to drive the Swedes out of the Delaware once and for all—which he did sixteen months later with the help of 200 soldiers and the warship *De Waegh*, chartered by the WIC from Amsterdam city. To repay this debt, the WIC granted Amsterdam all the land on the west side of the Delaware, and eventually the whole of the river, and here Amsterdam formed its own colony within the colony of New Netherland, called New Amstel, in the state of Delaware, today.

8

THE STUYVESANT YEARS:
WARS UPON WARS

But Petrus Stuyvesant's work was never done. No sooner had he set siege to the Swedes in their forts on the South River than word came that on September 15, 1655, huge numbers of Indians had gone on the rampage on Manhattan Island, heading straight for New Amsterdam, where the colonists' orchards were lush with ripe fruit.

The Second Dutch-Munsee War, or The Peach War

The peaches were particularly inviting, and an Indian stooped to gather some, whereupon the orchard's owner, Hendrick van Dijck, killed the thief, but not before Van Dijck was wounded in the chest by an arrow and another citizen threatened with an ax.[1]

In revenge, and as the Indians were preparing to leave the island, the *schout-fiscael* Cornelis van Tienhoven, Kieft's war-mongering councilor, and also a favorite of Petrus Stuyvesant, ordered the militia to fire on them, killing sixty or more. The Indians were swift to react. Over the next three days, they burned down all the houses in Cornelis Melyn's colony on Staten Island and destroyed all the farms on the west shore of the Hudson. They killed forty colonists, killed or took away cattle, burned 9,000 to 12,000 bushels of grain, and took a hundred women and children captive. Taking captives was partly to make up for their own slain family members in the First Dutch-Munsee War, according to one theory, and partly, according to another, to forestall a Dutch counterattack, reasoning that the Dutch would not retaliate while Dutch settlers were Munsee prisoners. It was two years before all the captives were returned and peace made.

Skirmishes and even slayings occurred in the period of peace that followed the Second Dutch-Munsee War, but Stuyvesant avoided another outright conflict by finding ways to appease the Indians and answer their demands, while at the same time persuading them to sell their land and move away. Although the Indians were coming to the conclusion that the European creep over their land was inevitable, the conclusion was painful and slow in coming. One of their tactics to delay the evil hour was to demand that the colonists repurchase land they had already bought once, or even twice.

The Third Dutch-Munsee War, or the Esopus War

The Third Dutch-Munsee War, also known as the Esopus War, broke out in 1659. The Esopus Indians lived along the Esopus Creek in the vicinity of today's Kingston, New York. In the lull in hostilities after the Peach War, Europeans who had fled the Esopus area during that time of war began to return. They were joined by new settlers attracted by the flat and fertile land and the convenience of the midpoint river access to the trade of both Fort Orange to the north and New Amsterdam to the south.

However, cultural differences emphasized by the physical proximity of settlers and Indians soon brought tensions to the fore again—tensions aggravated as they had been in the past by alcohol. With dreary predictability, the scenario played out. Traders gave alcohol to Indians in exchange for furs. Indians got drunk and took out their frustrations over their disappearing land on settlers. Stuyvesant tried diplomacy to calm both sides, but he demanded that Indians make reparation for their attacks and required Indians to "sell" ever more of their land to the settlers, even if they had sold the same land once or twice before, which happened.

He also demanded that the settlers move closer together for safety and build a fort to protect themselves at Wiltwijck (Kingston). But the Indians claimed the Wiltwijck land was theirs and that the Dutch had never paid them for it. And so it went.

As we saw in Chapter Four, land and to whom it belonged was at the bottom of the wars with the Indians. At first, this was not the case, because there was so much land at the beginning of the Dutch incursion that it did not occur to the Indians that a scarcity could develop, or that it could even disappear for their purposes. But once the fur trade was open to all, the European population began to soar, the forces of supply and demand came into play, and increasingly contentious encounters took place as a result.

There were other exacerbating causes as well: disputes "over the heavy-handedness of Dutch administrative practices; a shortage of food and, for many Indians, places to grow their crops; the exchange of prisoners taken in this or that conflict; the lucrative but risky trade in contraband; the business of selling alcohol to the Indians and its long-recognized and destructive effects; and the continued taking of Indian lands."[2] Finally, the gradual disappearance of beaver, first in the lower Hudson and then in the upper, led the Indians to "sell" their land to the colonists for the trade goods they had come to depend upon. And all was complicated by the Anglo-Dutch wars that caused disruption in the shipping of those trade goods to New Netherland.

The Role of Trade Goods

From the beginning, the Indians were enamored of European trade goods, and trade goods are linked to their demise. As Allen W. Trelease put it, from the time of Henry Hudson's visit in 1609, the Indians "were introduced to a new way of life, a culture entirely different from anything they had ever heard of"—or indeed dreamed existed. They came to want guns, alcohol, and western clothing "so badly," Trelease wrote, "that no price seemed too high to pay for them."[3] When the fur supply dried up, as it did in the 1650s, the Indians resorted to selling their land to get the trade goods they no longer wanted to live without.

Excavated sites tell the story. In the earliest trading periods, before the formation of the Dutch West India Company, the oldest excavated sites yield monochrome glass beads, brass kettles, iron axes, knives, awls, and brass bells. But soon more variety appears, no doubt in response to Indian demand: polychrome glass beads, woolen broadcloth, and ivory combs, followed by iron nails, spikes, scissors, adzes, and pottery fragments. Weapons, especially swords, make their appearance, as well as broken weapons, occasional gun parts, and musket balls. After 1624, high-quality colored beads in new styles, lead cloth seals, iron mouth harps, and copper kettles are found, joined soon by baked goods, shirts, stockings, duffel cloth, shoes, pipes, files, mirrors, mattocks, thimbles, buttons, and always of course guns, ammunition, and liquor.[4]

On the Esopus, tribal leaders sought to avoid conflict, but they emphasized the need for Stuyvesant to provide suitable gifts to the Indians in the interests of peace, reminding him that gift-giving in Indian culture was linked to the protocol for mitigating discord. Five hundred Indian warriors now gathered near Wiltwijck and publicly

8.1. Indian trade goods,
including glass beads, metal
Jesuit rings, lead musket
balls, the lock mechanism of
a flintlock musket, scissors,
a hatchet, a metal pot, and
arrow points fashioned from
kettle fragments.

*Department of Anthropology,
Research and Collections, New York
State Museum.*

73

busied themselves in the manufacture of bows and arrows, much to the unease of the settlers, who tried to scare them away by ambushing a group sleeping off the effects of brandy, killing one and wounding others. The Indians retaliated. The Dutch took refuge in the fort, where the Indians besieged them for more than three weeks.

Stuyvesant returned with armed volunteers to reinforce the fort, while Johannes La Montagne, now in charge at Fort Orange, attempted to negotiate peace with the help of friendly Mohawks and other Indians, but to no avail. It was not until the Hackensacks and other Munsees from the lower Hudson Valley exerted pressure on the Esopus Indians in the mid-Hudson that a peace was signed in the summer of 1660.

This truce lasted for only three years, when war broke out again, again with alcohol fueling the violence. By this time, the settlers had built a second village in the area, called Nieuwdorp (Hurley). In June 1663, the Esopus Indians attacked Nieuwdorp and burned it to the ground, killing most of the colonists, and then surged on to Wiltwijck, where they killed twenty settlers and captured forty-five.

Stuyvesant sailed back to Wiltwijck to try to secure the release of the prisoners, with the help of the Mohawks. One female prisoner was released. To free the rest, Captain Martin Cregier with a force of 210 set upon the villages of the Esopus and their fort, which they burned along with the Indians' stockpiled grains and corn. They then pursued the Indians into the interior, where they destroyed what they could find of their possessions and killed or captured more than thirty Esopus. Over the fall and into the spring of 1664, the Indians gradually returned their captives, and in May a peace agreement was reached again, with the help of other Munsees.

By 1664, the Indians and Europeans had occupied the same land for forty years. By this time, the Munsees in the Hudson Valley had long come to depend on European goods for survival, and they had, reluctantly, also come to accept that the Europeans were among them to stay. Further, European diseases had taken their toll, so that the Indians were losing ground in more ways than one. Their numbers were declining, and their land was disappearing into the ravening maw of the Europeans. But, again, it was 1664, and Dutch rule was about to come to an end, although not because of the Munsees.

Peace Fleeting, Wars a Constant

If it seems as if war was a constant between the colonists and the

Indians in New Netherland, Robert Grumet's "Timeline" for the years 1640 to 1664 confirms this impression, with at least fourteen references to specific outbreaks and attacks during this twenty-four-year period, an average of one bloody conflict every one and a half years. The timeline does not take into account wars that fell outside of it, such as the three Anglo-Powhatan Wars in Virginia or the Pequot War in Connecticut, French attacks on Mohawks and Hurons, or wars among the Indians themselves, news of all of which stressed out the citizens of New Netherland. War was endemic. As Grumet put it, "A seemingly endless succession of wars and rumors of wars rolled over the Hudson and Delaware Valleys like a smothering artillery barrage during the final two decades of Dutch rule."[5]

The Iroquois League, comprising in this period the Five Nations, Mohawk, Oneida, Onandago, Cayuga, and Seneca Indians, was also in a state of chronic warfare in the seventeenth century. But Iroquoian hostility toward the French and their Indian allies was not a simple case of intending to dominate the beaver economy, as commonly held. Rather, according to one historian who has closely examined primary documents, it was of a more complicated cast with the goals of replenishing their populations, safeguarding their hunting territories, protecting their homes, gaining honor, and seeking revenge.[6]

Finally, native peoples should not be viewed as mere victims of colonial ambitions. They had their own agendas, and whether peltry was their main goal or not, they were willing agents in the fur trade. They understood well the colonists' desire for furs, and they entered into the beaver economy with their own profits in mind, not hesitating to up the ante when it was to their advantage, or to play one buyer off against another, whether Dutch, French, English, or fellow Natives.

Indians' View of Land

The way the Indians viewed land and the way their view changed when the Dutch appeared in their midst in the 1600s is central to an understanding of the history of the warfare that occurred.

Adriaen van der Donck observed that "wind, stream, bush, field, sea, beach, and riverside are open and free to everyone of every nation with which the Indians are not embroiled in open conflict. All those are free to enjoy and move about such places as though they were born there." In other words, the Indians understood a concept of "use right" to land based on how it was used and for what purpose. As

William A. Starna has written, the Indians "lacked entirely a concept of land ownership and did not conceive of anything approaching the jurisdiction and control assumed by Europeans. . . . The world of these native people was absent metes and bounds."[7]

But the Dutch liked metes and bounds. It was their belief that the natives owned the land and that they, the Dutch, must obtain it from them by legal purchase. The 1625 Instructions to Verhulst and the Freedoms and Exemptions of 1629 outlined the procedure for obtaining it, which entailed giving the Indians trading goods to induce them to give up ownership of their land without forcing them or taking possession by craft or fraud.

We cannot know for sure whether the Indians understood what they were doing when they signed deeds conveying their land to the Dutch, or as Starna points out, whether they even had a legal right to sell the land in the first place. But what is clear is that the Indians were insistent on possessing the trade goods the Dutch offered, and the Dutch were insistent in wanting (and needing) the land the Indians possessed. There was thus a *quid pro quo* that both were satisfied with—for a time.

There is little evidence that the colonists cheated the Indians out of their land, but there was a growing awareness on the part of the Indians that the Europeans were going to keep on coming and there was nothing they could do about it. They also came to realize that there was a finite amount of land and other critical resources to be had, and a seemingly infinite demand for them by the settlers. All of these understandings caused anger to develop and wars to arise. The Indians, weakened by disease, alcohol, and insufficient technological knowhow to manufacture the goods they wanted, lost those wars.

From Trading Post to Colony

Despite the violence that marred it, the Stuyvesant administration was by far the most successful in New Netherland's history. Lasting for seventeen years from 1647 to 1664, Stuyvesant's tenure saw the transition from a society peopled by WIC soldiers and employees, fur traders, young single men, enslaved Africans, and Native Americans to one where families with children and servants, tradesmen, artisans, and merchants began to predominate. New Netherland made the final evolution during Stuyvesant's administration from a trading post to a family-oriented colony undergirded by agricultural and mercantile pursuits, with a centralized government and an admirable judicial system, both of which were useful to the English when they took over in 1664 and were thus retained.

The transition was hastened by the fall of Dutch Brazil to Portugal in 1654. The WIC now redirected its resources in men and treasure, which had been vastly wasted in trying to maintain New Holland in Brazil, to its neglected colony on the Hudson. The fall of New Sweden the following year also contributed to the growth and stability of the total population of New Netherland, for Stuyvesant allowed the Swedes and Finns to remain in their villages on the Delaware as part of what he called the "Swedish nation" within New Netherland, which policy in turn encouraged more Scandinavians to emigrate. Still, the total population of New Netherland in 1654 is estimated to have been between a mere 2,000 and a maximum of 3,500. It would grow to close to 9,000 within the next decade, a remarkable indication of the colony's appeal to settlers who wanted to better their lives in the bountiful Eden portrayed in the promotional literature that flourished in the Netherlands.

To Be Clean, Orderly, Strong, and Moral

For Stuyvesant the disorder, uncleanliness, and stench that confronted him when he stepped off the boat indicated that even a population as small as 2,000 required close supervision and direction. From the start he governed, famously, with ordinances and promulgations, edicts, decrees, and instructions to clean up the place. New rules gushed from his order-obsessed mind covering everything from the citizens' custom of throwing their garbage out the window to land where it may, to the delight of the roving pigs and hogs who scavenged after it where they might.

He ordered fences to be built to confine roaming beasts, streets to be laid out, and privies to be emptied or replaced when their contents overflowed. He prohibited wooden chimneys and thatched roofs, he appointed fire wardens and chimney sweeps. He set up an Orphan Masters' Court to safeguard the rights and funds of those left without parents (and, somewhat contradictorily, imported more orphans from Amsterdam as apprentices and servants). He organized the rattle watch, set up the city's first hospital, instituted a Poor Law, established a rudimentary post office. It was the seventeenth-century version of government in your face. It was Ben Franklin before there was Ben Franklin.

8.2 "Manhattan, 1660," by
L. F. Tantillo. The artist's
conjectural view based on
the 1660 survey known as
the Castello Plan redrawn
to agree with a precise
1890s street survey.

L. F. Tantillo works.

He decreed that all real-estate transactions required his approval and a proper recording by the secretary on his council. He set up a weekly municipal market on Mondays where meat, bacon, butter, cheese, and other products of the farm could be bought and sold, as well as a Saturday market for the convenience of the "country people" on the East River beach, where farmers from across the water sold their wares from their boats moored in the Heere Gracht canal. He ordered a cattle market to be set up for forty days every fall to which men and their livestock came from as far away as the east end of Long Island.

He advised the Court of Burgomasters and Schepens to see to it that weights and measures were properly inspected; inspectors were appointed to make sure that bakers and bolters were following the laws regarding quality and weight; and a similar oversight was directed at tavern keepers and tapsters. He initiated the burgher right, decreeing that itinerant merchants, known as Scotch traders, could not sell their wares unless they had "fire and light," that is, a proper dwelling house, for it was the practice of these seasonal traders to buy furs from the Indians in Beverwijck over the normal retail price, which they could afford to do as they did not maintain homes in the colony or pay taxes, and sell same at discount, destroying the markets for legal inhabitants. He turned his attention to the wampum situation, the main currency of the colony, where inflation was occurring because of bad quality and increased quantity as the New England colonies began to coin their own money and unload their wampum on New Netherland, and his council established rules for wampum's quality—and fines for breaking them.

And he established a slave market in New Amsterdam. Up to this time, and starting in 1626, the WIC had brought enslaved Africans captured on the high seas to New Amsterdam as a source of hard labor in building the community's infrastructure. By 1639, they were housed in a camp on the East River a few miles north of the city, seen on the Manatus Map of that year. Meanwhile, the WIC was transporting tens of thousands of Africans to the Caribbean tobacco and sugar plantations a year, where after a period of "seasoning," some were resold to slavers who then marketed them to plantation owners in Virginia, the Chesapeake, and New Netherland. Stuyvesant's idea was to import them directly from Angola in West Africa to increase New Amsterdam's growing need for a labor force and to assist new settlers in building up the hinterland, always a goal of New Netherland's directors to reinforce the WIC's claim to the territory and to forestall more

English encroachment.

The first slave ship arrived in New Amsterdam harbor on September 15, 1655, with about 300 Africans aboard. This cargo sold for a tidy sum, alerting Company and colonists alike to the profits inherent in the business. The next year another ship and subsequently two more arrived with hundreds of African human beings stacked like cord wood within the hulls, men and women ignorant of, but probably suspecting, the cruel fate that awaited them. By the late 1650s, according to Oliver Rink, Company contracts and charter agreements for slave ships sailing directly to New Netherland had become so commonplace that forms were printed that "left blanks for inserting the name of the ship and her captain as well as the specific destinations on the West African coast where gangs of slaves could be picked up."[8] Many historians, including Africans, have documented that these "gangs" were rounded up for sale by their own people, who also found the trade profitable. In 1664, when the English took over, it is estimated that there were about 600 enslaved people in New Netherland, or between 6 and 8 percent of the population.

Like everyone else in town when there was a big project to accomplish, such as constructing the wall, the male slaves joined the Europeans to carry it out. But male slaves not only worked on New Amsterdam's infrastructure, building roads and the fort and the wall, they repaired same, worked as stevedores in the shipyards, waited on soldiers, sowed and reaped in the fields, chopped wood, hauled water, and labored on the dunghills, while their women cooked and cleaned for their owners, did their laundry, kept their fires going, and cared for their owners' children and their own children in between.

Abhorrent as it was, the trade in humans was way second to the trade in commodities: furs, tobacco, timber, and grain. With free trade established when the WIC gave up its monopoly in 1639, private merchants in bustling Amsterdam took over the transatlantic markets with enthusiasm, partnering with private merchants in New Amsterdam. Oliver Rink has described in detail the role of Amsterdam merchant firms in offering credit to Manhattan merchants and in establishing the credit process as to formal written contracts and the means to enforce them by appeal to Director and council in cases of default and debt.[9]

The system worked fairly well at first, but it worked better after the creation of the municipal government in 1653, for now the merchants, through the Court of Burgomasters and Schepens, had more control over the written instruments on which their credit was based, rather than leaving it to the Director General and his council to guarantee their debts or settle their suits. Historian Dennis Maika has described one of these tools used in special cases as "hypotheca mortgages," formal bonds representing sworn agreements between debtor and creditor in which the debtor pledged collateral, usually a piece of property, as security for the loan. Both parties benefitted from this system. The debtor could retain possession of his property for the duration of the loan, and the creditor had a formal written acknowledgment of his loan that would stand up in court to assure settlement in case of default.[10]

Taking a look again at "*Nieu Amsterdam*," the copper engraving, Plate 5.1 on page 45, we see in the midground a busy harbor, c. 1653. Oliver Rink has documented that 131 cargo-laden vessels sailed into and out of this harbor from 1645 to 1664, an average of 6.5 per year, with the smallest number, one, in 1645, and the largest number, eleven, in 1664. Petrus Stuyvesant must have been proud of his part in accomplishing an atmosphere of safety and order that encouraged both settlement and trade. It was seven years into his tenure, and New Amsterdam, indeed New Netherland, was satisfyingly on the rise.

But a closer look tells another story, for the busy harbor where three large transatlantic vessels wait to be loaded or unloaded, suggesting happy profits for their owners and investors, is somewhat deceptive. Maritime trade was fraught with perils. It was periodically disrupted by wars, and when this happened insurance rates soared, as did interest rates on bonds. In the first Anglo-Dutch War, 1652-1654, for instance, the interest rates on bonds reached as high as 49 percent in 1653.[11] Storms and shipwrecks, spoilage and spoliation, piracy and plundering all took their toll, as did the various English Navigation Acts that attempted to prohibit foreign goods and products from entering English ports except in English ships, closed English coastal water to foreign fishermen, and required foreign ships to salute them when meeting on the sea. The Acts, intended to protect the English shipping and fishing industries from the superior capabilities of the Dutch, were hard to enforce, but they represented annoying interference in Dutch maritime activities.

Such impediments, along with the expenses of shipbuilding and fitting, labor, commissions, and opportunity cost drove the cost of shipping to New Netherland to about 50 percent above the price for the goods purchased in the Netherlands. To spread the risk among investors, the Dutch used an ancient form of limited-liability financing known as "bottomry bonds," loans secured by the bottom or keel of the ship, the idea being that if the voyage failed and the merchant defaulted on the bond, the investors could sell the cargo to recoup their investment. But if the cargo was at the bottom of the sea, all lost all.[12]

Another strategy was to spread the risk among investors through the subcontracting of bottomry bonds, which allowed more investors to be involved for smaller amounts. But this had its drawbacks, too, for debtors sometimes reneged on their promise to pay back sums owed to their creditors, and they sometimes died, in which case the creditor had to pursue the debtor's heirs through the courts.

To illustrate the perils, no example is more stunning than the fate of the *Princess Amelia*, a ship owned by the WIC on which Dominie Everardus Bogardus and Director Willem Kieft sailed to the Netherlands in 1647 to bring their feud before the authorities in The Hague and to defend their actions from their critics' charges. In a case of mistaken piloting, the *Princess Amelia* sank off the coast of Wales, where most of its cargo, estimated at between 14,000 and 16,000 beaver pelts and 200,000 pounds of red dyewood, "was taken up and purloyned away" by locals for a total loss between ship and cargo estimated at about 400,000 Dutch guilders.[13] Eighty-six passengers, including many discharged soldiers returning home from Brazil after a stopover in New Netherland, minister, director, their papers, and the ship's papers were all lost, underscoring the intricate and entwined roles of the States General of the Dutch Republic, the Dutch West India Company, the Reformed Dutch Church, and the risk in treasure and in person to investors in maritime and merchant activity in New Netherland.

9

CHURCH, STATE, AND PETRUS STUYVESANT

It has often been said that in New Netherland, profits came first, the colony was built on greed, and religion was only an afterthought. This is a misunderstanding. As noted in Chapter Five, in the seventeenth century religion was an integral part of people's lives to an extent hard to imagine in our secularized world today. In the Netherlands in the seventeenth century, and so in New Netherland, church and state shared a mutual ambition and responsibility to develop an orderly society whose moral code was based on Biblical precepts. Working hand in hand, the government expected the church to uphold the government's laws, and the church expected the government to support its ecclesiastical goals. The idea of the separation of church and state was an idea whose time was far in the future.[1]

Duties of Church and State

Rules drawn up in 1619 to govern the Reformed Dutch Church state it this way: Christian magistrates (and all magistrates were Christians in those days) have a duty to encourage the worship of God, to recommend religion by their example, and to protect the members of the community in the full and regular exercise of religious liberty. Likewise, church officials—ministers, elders, and deacons, who together formed the consistory—must instill in all their congregations "obedience, love, and homage" toward their rulers.[2]

The state, too, had its rules. The instructions given to Willem Verhulst, New Netherland's first director, in 1625 emphasized his responsibility to see that divine service was held both on board ship and on the land, as well as to instruct the Indians in Christianity, and in general to uphold the name and word of God.[3] Although the state was the stronger partner in the relationship, in the seventeenth century both State and Church believed that they were mutually benefited by advancing the "true Christian religion" (by which they meant Dutch Reformed Calvinism), thus fostering a law-abiding and harmonious society with God's word as its guide.

WIC and Church

The directors of the West India Company in the Netherlands were thoroughly involved in the affairs of the church in New Netherland. Acting on the advice of the Classis of Amsterdam, they appointed Reformed ministers to New Netherland and in some cases paid their salaries. In other cases, the local government oversaw the collection of funds for the minister's salary or paid it out of its own resources. With the "laudable customs of the fatherland" as their model, local officials drew up the instructions and rules for the schoolmaster, usually a lay preacher, charging him to teach the children the "Christian prayers, commandments, baptism, Lord's supper and the questions with answers of the [Heidelberg] catechism."[4] This is not only how children learned the precepts of the faith, it was also how they learned to read and thus to function in a world where literacy was essential to trade and commerce— again a goal that suited the needs of both church and state.

Local officials saw to the building of the church and supervised repairs to it as needed through the office of churchmaster appointed by the court, and they tried to ensure that the people had the benefit of an ordained minister at all times. When Dominie Johannes Megapolensis wished to return to the Netherlands in 1649, Director General Petrus Stuyvesant and his council could not accept his decision, for he was needed "for the glory of God, the upbuilding of His church and the salvation of men" in New Netherland.[5] Megapolensis loyally changed his plans and stayed on until his death twenty-one years later.

Oaths, Prayers, and Proclamations

The printed records of New Netherland make this hand-in-hand relationship between church and state very clear. From its opening prayer in 1653, for instance, to the oath of its officials, to its daily dealings with the people, the records of the Court of Burgomasters and Schepens reveal that religion was no afterthought in this community. It was an integral part of everyday life. Upon taking office, court officials took an oath to protect the "pure and true Christian Religion as taught in the Netherland Churches conformably to the Word of God and the order of the Synod of Dordrecht" of 1619.[6]

The prayer with which the court opened its first session in 1653 is a succinct distillation of Reformed theology as found in the Heidelberg Catechism, one of the six doctrinal standards of the Reformed Dutch Church.[7] In a manner unimaginable in today's strictly secular halls of government, the prayer began by invoking God and acknowledging God as the merciful father in heaven to whom the officials owed thanks for creating them, receiving them in Christ as allies, and making them the rulers in New Netherland—even though they are mere miserable and undeserving mortals unfit to carry out their charge unless He assists them.

In the prayer, this God, the fountain of all good, is a kindly figure more concerned with enabling the members of the court to do his work faithfully and honestly than with consternating them with ideas of eternal damnation. They beg him to enlighten them, so that they can tell right from wrong, truth from lies, and make just decisions fair to rich and poor, friends and enemies, and inhabitants and strangers alike, showing favor to none and taking gifts from none. They ask that he keep their hearts from greed, let them listen patiently to the litigants who come before them, condemn no one lightly, and use the power he has given them for the benefit of the authorities of the church, the protection of the good, and the punishment of the bad. The idea that undergirds this prayer, that the court is carrying out God's will for his creation in New Netherland, is striking—as is the vision it incorporates of the just and fair community its leaders hoped to achieve.

An Angry God

The idea that God will visit his anger on his creation in New Netherland is also striking in the official proclamations periodically announcing days of prayer, fasting, and thanksgiving. This is particularly so of the proclamations of Petrus Stuyvesant, which are sprinkled through the records of both court and council. He declared perhaps the most ringing of them in April 1648 at a time when calamities of various types were visiting Europe, Brazil, the Caribbean Islands, Curaçao, and even places in North America—calamities brought on, the document declared, because "the Holy and Almighty God of Israel" was angry at his people for their sins.[8] They must repent; otherwise, the same wrath will surely be visited on them.

9.1 "Petrus Stuyve-
sant," stained glass
window, St. Mark's
Church in-the-Bowery,
1903.

*Photo by Dr. Laurence
Simpson. Courtesy of the
St. Mark's Historic Landmark
Fund.*

Stuyvesant set aside the first Wednesday of every month as a special day to ask God to divert his anger from New Netherland, grant the inhabitants health and fertile seasons, turn aside storms, favor their navigation, industry, and commerce, and keep the light of the holy Gospel burning both in New Netherland and in their "dear fatherland." As did all his proclamations, this one asked that God give him and his council wisdom to decide nothing but what will serve his glory, their salvation, and the welfare of the country.

These are no mere pious words taken out of a printed book. They are composed to address the local situation, in full belief that God is present among them, ready to punish them or bless them, as their behavior warrants. In February 1660 the council's proclamation of a day of fasting and prayer refers to the "Hot fevers, heavy Rheums, Dizziness of the head and many more diseases" God had visited on the people of New Netherland for their transgressions. It describes the threats of encroachments "on our long possessed Lands, Streams and Rivers" by their neighbors, and the "Murders and Burnings by Barbarous Natives that God hath so mitigated and directed" that the worst did not happen, even though they deserved it. They beg God to keep and maintain them and "this early budding Province in His Fatherly Protection" against all those who seek its ruin and to favor the rulers of the land with knowledge, wisdom, prudence, and holiness that they might promote the welfare of the country and the prosperity of the good inhabitants.[9]

Heidelberg Catechism

These various items—the oath of office, the court's opening prayer, and the texts of the proclamations of days of prayer, fasting, and thanksgiving—all touch on doctrinal points that would have been familiar to people raised from childhood on the Heidelberg Catechism, the Reformed Church's principal teaching tool.

A scholar has described the Heidelberg Catechism as "intensely Calvinistic."[10] To the modern mind, this phrase may evoke images of zealotry, the controversial ideas of predestination and limited atonement, fire and brimstone, and an insistence on moral perfection. But Calvinism has another side to it that should also be recognized. As expressed in the Heidelberg Catechism, it has a charitable, conciliatory, even lenient side, a feat its authors accomplished by omitting any mention of eternal damnation and stressing that faith, not foreordained decrees of predestined eternal fate, was necessary for salvation.

It is remarkable to see how this charitable tone also guided the actions of the New Amsterdam Court of Burgomasters and Schepens as it sought to bring unity and order to an often chaotic community. Both church and state, in this trading community on this wild frontier, were hard put to stamp their standards of propriety on the inhabitants, and the records of the court reveal the government's endless attempts to deal with its Sabbath-breaking, hard-drinking, brawling, cheating, adulterous, sneaky, and thieving citizens. This is the side of New Amsterdam that has often been played up by historians, as has the image of a harsh Calvinism intent on spoiling the people's fun and forcing them into rigid molds of good behavior.

But noteworthy is how the Court of Burgomasters and Schepens, as well as the other courts, bent over backward to be patient, lenient, just, and fair. It was ever hopeful of reconciliation, ever putting its faith in arbitration over confrontation, always helpful to the helpless, and sometimes willing to discount or even overlook ("wink at") the deficiencies of those who came before it. The forbearing behavior of the magistrates suggests that these government officials were attempting to practice the kinder, gentler side of Dutch Calvinist doctrine as found in the Catechism with which they were so familiar. It suggests that the images of the kind of society they imagined ruling over, as revealed in the oath of office, the court's opening prayers, and the proclamations of periodic days of prayer, fasting, and thanksgiving were the embodiment of actual deeply held ideals.

A Lenient Court

The greatest part of the cases coming before the Court of Burgomasters and Schepens fell into three categories: those involving matters of credit and debt, misunderstandings over contract terms, and cases of slander and insult. The burgomasters and schepens decided many cases on the merits, once they examined the facts, but if the facts were obscure they almost invariably appointed two arbitrators to determine the outcome, or a pair of experts to go out and view a disputed boundary or complaints of shoddy workmanship or spoiled produce. Many litigants came to agreement on their own, declaring in public that, "having become reconciled, they will remain good friends henceforth." Or they "will no longer remember their foregoing dispute, and they settle with each other equitably and make payment." In a case where a plaintiff's

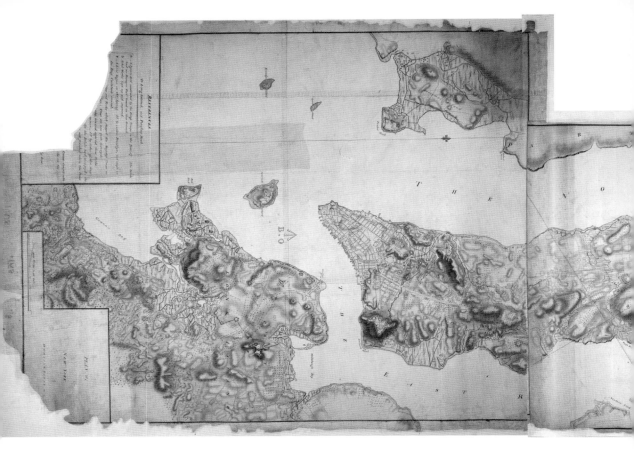

property was restored, she declared herself "willing to forgive the defendant, and never to trouble her again"—outcomes that echo the tone of conciliation and concord valued by the court.[11]

The court was patient, allowing weeks and even months for a debtor to pay what he owed, giving parties "time to think the matter over," urging the litigants to "agree together as friends" until the defendant could scrape his funds together. And it was lenient. A defendant was found in default, "but for reasons, he is excused." Another, though guilty, was "allowed to pursue his business as before, inasmuch as he is burthened with a houseful of children." The burgomasters showed leniency toward a woman unable to afford the fee for her burgher right, and to a widow having trouble paying a debt. They suspended the burger-right fee for another woman in straits. They agreed "to wink at" an old man's inability to pay his fees, to wait for another man's payment, to reduce the amount another must pay for his fire-bucket dues, and to excuse another who was finding it difficult to pay his rattle-watch dues, "as he has not so much." A woman who could not pay her rattle-watch dues was promised "that she should not be spoken to about it very soon." One guilty party "shall, for this time," be excused from banishment, provided he asks the court's pardon and promises to behave himself.[12]

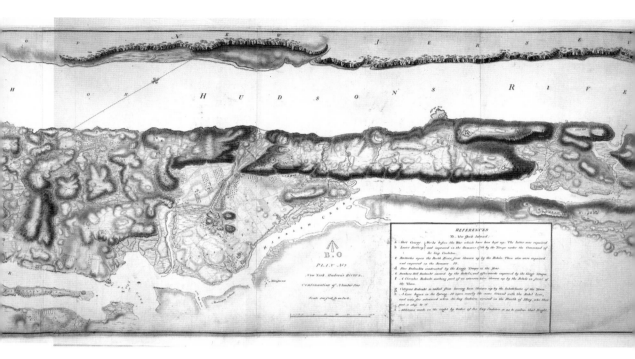

We have heard of compassionate conservativism. New Netherland had what might be called compassionate Calvinism, for underlying the decisions of the Court of Burgomasters and Schepens was a foundation of Christian precepts: love your neighbor, be peaceable, turn the other cheek, forgive and forget, show mercy. The image of a wished-for ideal society threads through their records in the recurring phrases with which the officials hope for the "contentment and security of the Burghery," "what is best for the public good," the "peace and maintenance of unity," the "quiet, unity and welfare of the country in general." And just as they understood that church and state worked hand in hand to achieve these goals, so they also believed that that "justice [which] is the foundation of the republic" was based on "divine and human law," that the "law of God was the general basis of the law."

If It Were Properly Fortified . . .

The society they hoped to create in New Netherland in the image of the fatherland was doomed. A letter of February 1664 from burgomasters and schepens to the Director General and council begging for help in fortifying New Amsterdam against the English puts the society they had served since the court's inception eleven years earlier in poignant perspective: "This capital, where your Honours' good and faithful inhabitants, mostly Dutchmen, have at their own expense built so many fine houses . . . should be properly fortified . . . [so] that it might cause malevolent neighbours to fear it." If it were properly fortified, they go on, the city could be a place "where its 10,000 inhabitants might grow into a great people," and a place that in time and with God's blessing "might even become a place of refuge, if our Netherlands should be visited by cruel wars." It might even become the "granary for our Fatherland in case of failure of the Eastern crops or a prohibition of trade by the Northern kings and princes," and the "staple of commerce for our Fatherland."[13] When the end came, it came fast. A few months later, improved fortifications unbuilt, the little colony fell to the English.

The vision of New Netherland as a refuge in time of war or economic crisis at home, a breadbasket, an Edenic land capable of supplying the fatherland with manna in its time of need, was in line with the other religious metaphors its leaders used for it as a just society based on God's word. Religion was no afterthought in New Netherland. It was woven into the civic fabric and inseparable from it.

Petrus Stuyvesant: His Learning Curve

The ironic thing is that Petrus Stuyvesant, serious, practicing Christian and Company man that he was, took his instructions from the WIC to keep the Reformed Dutch Church in a position of unassailable authority so to heart that he has come to be remembered as intolerant and uncompassionate. This was just the opposite of what was needed in the rough little frontier communities that he governed, where "eighteen languages were spoken," and where men and women of all nationalities and faiths had emigrated in hope of finding a home and a future free of prejudice, poverty, and strife.

Jews from Brazil

Jews are a case in point. At the fall of New Holland in Brazil in January 1654, Jews who had settled in Recife evacuated and fled, some to English Surinam, some to Amsterdam, some to other parts of the Caribbean, and twenty-three Sephardic Jews to New Netherland, bereft of their property and owing the WIC money for their passage. Soon, Stuyvesant wrote to the directors in Amsterdam to complain of these refugees, stating that he had asked them, "a deceitful race," to depart. As historian Noah Gelfand has put it, "For Stuyvesant, a staunch Calvinist who was already having trouble maintaining order in the pluralistic religious culture of New Netherland that included Lutherans, Puritans, Mennonites, and Catholics, the addition of these particular Jews was not a welcomed development."[14]

The Sephardic community in Amsterdam petitioned the WIC to ensure the rights of their compatriots to live and conduct business in New Amsterdam, as they were allowed to do in Amsterdam, and the WIC responded positively, writing to Stuyvesant to allow them to remain in the city, provided they not became a burden to the community or the company, but be supported by their own. Stuyvesant obeyed, but he attempted to exclude them from militia service, tax them for their defense, curtail their trade activities, and prevent them from settling in certain areas of the city. They lingered for a while, but were gone by the time of the English takeover in 1664.

Quakers from England

Stuyvesant also denied Lutherans the right to worship in public or to have a clergyman to lead them, and he was equally appalled by Papists, Mennonites, Puritans, and Independents, as well as atheists, but he reserved his special fury for the Society of Friends, or Quakers, a troop of whom made an appearance in New Amsterdam harbor on August 6, 1657. They were bound for Rhode Island, "where all the cranks of New England retire," according to the Reformed ministers, but they left several behind, including two women. The women soon began to quake and go into a frenzy, crying out and praying, and astounding all who came to stare at them. The *schout* threw them in jail and had their fellow Quaker, one Robert Hodgson, severely whipped for proselytizing on Long Island.

Hodgson was soon joined by other Quakers in the town of Vlissingen (Flushing) on Long Island, and before long, in defiance of the rule that only the Reformed religion was allowed public worship, the Quakers were meeting openly and with the open support of the Flushing people, notably *schout* Tobias Feake, Flushing town clerk Edward Hart, and John Bowne, who hosted Quaker meetings at his home.

In 1662 Stuyvesant and council banished Bowne from New Netherland for this offense. Bowne promptly sailed for the Netherlands to deliver a petition (a characteristically Dutch legal form) to the Amsterdam Chamber of the WIC demanding religious toleration for the Quakers in accord with Article 13 of the Union of Utrecht, which states that "each person shall remain free, especially in his religion, and that no

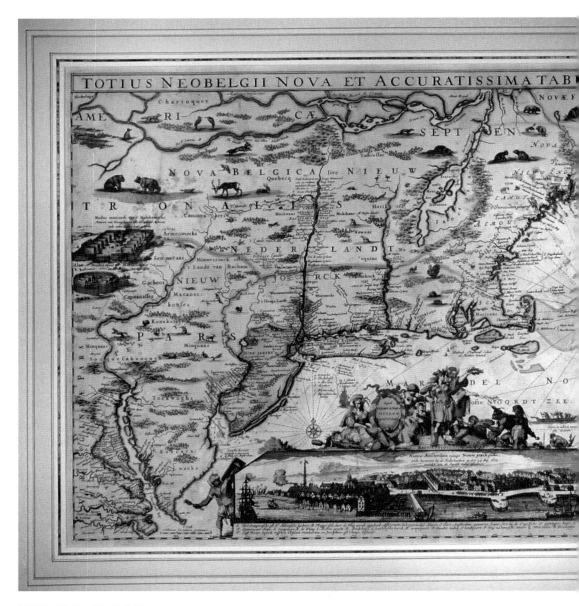

9.3 "Restitution View" of New Amsterdam, 1673, in the inset.

Bert Twaalfhoven Collection, Fordham University Library, Bronx, New York.

94

one shall be persecuted or investigated because of their religion."

If the "law of love, peace and liberty" in the Netherlands extends to Jews, Muslims and Gypsies, the petition asked, does it not extend to all in Christ Jesus? The answer was yes. The WIC rejected Stuyvesant's policy of exclusion and granted religious toleration to the Quakers, as long as they gave no offense to their neighbors and did not oppose the government. Known as the Flushing Remonstrance, this petition, signed by thirty-one Flushing residents, is regarded by some historians as a step toward the freedom of religion guaranteed in the U.S. Constitution. (Bowne's home is today open to the public as the Bowne House Historical Society honoring his dedication to the principle of religious toleration.)[15]

Stuyvesant was not just being blindly intolerant or prejudiced. He truly believed that uniformity in religion was the basis for a community's stability and order and that it was his duty to ward off dissenters and potential rabble-rousers. As in all he did, he sought after what he thought was best for the people, the Company, the colony. He sought the clean, the strong, the safe, the orderly, and the good. The lesson he had to learn was that he did not always know what was best. Often, the people knew better than he what was good for them.

As with the public works he undertook to better the community, so he tried to perfect public morals. He was a fixer and a doer in both realms, and he had plenty of things to fix, especially when the population began to grow by leaps and bounds in the late 1650s.

As historians have written of him, he was a "puritan at heart and a disciplinarian by profession, [and] tried by all possible means to force his bawdy citizens to live according to Christian rules."[16] The Reformed Dutch Church ministers were active participants in his never-ending efforts to regulate brewers, tavern keepers, and tapsters, to eradicate such "popish" holidays as Shrove Tuesday, to punish those caught "pulling the goose," a nasty game in which a greased goose was tied between two poles, with riders galloping past it and trying to tear its head off, and those having sex with Indians, premarital sex, or committing adultery.

His Sabbatarian policies aimed to get the people into church twice on Sunday, with no frivolity in between, no pleasure parties in boats, carts, or wagons, no tapping, fishing, hunting, handicrafts, or business "be it in houses, cellars, shops, ships, yachts, or on the streets," no picnicking, or playing board games or ball. Still, the people ignored him, as his repetitive ordinances and decrees attest. Those who believed in keeping the Sabbath holy did so. Others did as they pleased. Despite court, council, church, and director general, the New Amsterdam public was of a live-and-let-live frame of mind, a characteristic of the city that has survived the centuries.

On His Bouwerie

In August of 1664, during a time of peace between the Netherlands and England, an English fleet of three frigates under the command of Richard Nicolls appeared in New York harbor and demanded that the colony surrender. It was fifty-five years since Henry Hudson had sailed into the same waters and started the whole process.

Petrus Stuyvesant strenuously objected to the illegal act, but the colonists were unwilling to put up a fight, and in fact they regarded themselves as incapable of doing so, because of their small numbers, the weakened condition of the fort, and their sneaking suspicions that the English on Long Island would soon show up on Manhattan with looting and plundering in mind. The die was cast. Even one of Petrus Stuyvesant's sons was among the seventeen colonists who urged him, in writing, to surrender.

On his *bouwerie*, in the mansion house he had built for himself, he signed the Articles of Transfer, and without any fanfare New Netherland became New York and New Jersey.

Stuyvesant was ordered to Amsterdam to explain to the WIC and then to the States General why he had lost the colony. He defended himself well, pointing out as politely as possible that the WIC directors had not supported him as he had begged them to do countless times— and as they should have done if they had wanted the colony to succeed. The Nineteen did not find his explanations for surrendering the colony satisfactory and accused him of incompetence and cowardice, which angered him no end, for he believed the opposite, that the colony would have succeeded under his administration if the WIC had not been so stingy with its funds and its soldiers.

The process of defending himself took three years, both for the obstacles the WIC set for him and also because the States General was preoccupied with military matters, the Republic at the time being in the midst of the Second Anglo-Dutch War (1665-1667). In fact, it is clear that imperial concerns undergirded the context of the takeover, although the empire was the rising British empire, whereas at the beginning of New Netherland's existence it had been Spain's. For the English, the takeover of New Netherland in 1664 was, as Jaap Jacobs has written, a "means of inspiring awe in the anti-monarchist New England colonies. The display of kingly might was intended to facilitate the expansion of respect for the throne" throughout North America.[17] The Atlantic Ocean from the Irish Sea to North America to South America, enfolding the Caribbean, and flowing back to Europe by way of Africa was the watery stage now dominated by England on which the dramas of the next century would be played out.

The Second Anglo-Dutch War ended with the Dutch victorious at the Battle of the Medway in June 1667, and a tired and homesick Stuyvesant made his way back across the Atlantic.

In the end he was not charged with any malfeasance, nor had he committed any, and he returned to his farm in the Out Ward, north of the wall, to live out his days in the place he loved, with his beloved wife. He died in 1672 and thus did not live to see the happy day in 1673 when the Dutch recovered New Netherland from the English—for fifteen months. The so-called Restitution View, the inset in Plate 9.3, made to celebrate the restoration of Dutch rule, depicts a handsome little town that New Amsterdamers could be proud of and for whose flourishing Petrus Stuyvesant was largely responsible.

His farm, which he had purchased from the Company in 1648, was originally of about 300 acres but over the years he had purchased surrounding lots and taken over abandoned ones, and it eventually became 550 acres, an irregularly shaped parcel stretching from present Fifth Street to Twenty-third Street and from the Bowery or Fourth Avenue to the East River. Parts of it were swampy, and he allocated many of his resources to draining it. In fact, he testified that he had improved this land by fencing, damming, and raising up some abandoned lots, "at great cost and labour, out of the water and swamp, with about eight or nine thousand [wagon] loads of sand."[18]

On Plate 9.2, the very detailed British Headquarters Map, c. 1782-1783, the Sand Hills of the lower East Side stand out, a major natural geological phenomenon estimated to be 100 feet in elevation.[19] They were huge, and they were in Petrus Stuyvesant's way. As he had dismantled and moved Fort Nassau down the Delaware, so moving 9,000 wagonloads of sand around his farm was no big deal. Such came naturally to the phenomenon known as Petrus Stuyvesant, doer and fixer, builder of colonies, creator of public order, mover of Mother Earth.

10

THE PEOPLE OF NEW NETHERLAND

As we know from the Manatus Map of 1639 and the copper engraving, Plate 5.1, *"Nieu Amsterdam"* of about 1653, social class existed in New Netherland. Government officials and clergy were at the top of the ladder, followed by merchants, then skilled artisans, then unskilled labor, and at the bottom enslaved peoples and Indians. Though forced to live in the European society, the Africans had a social system of their own with layers and distinctions that historians still little understand. The same is true of the Native Americans, whose multiple cultures are slowly being uncovered.

"Nieu Amsterdam"

Let's take another look at the copper engraving, Plate 5.1, *"Nieu Amsterdam,"* for it teems with information about New Amsterdam and its people. It is even prophetic, offering glimpses of what the future city would become: a crowded and bustling metropolis where trade would be king, swarming with people of all classes, ethnicities, religions, and races and characterized by mixtures of every sort: buyers and sellers, Europeans, Africans, and Indians, south and north, risk and reward, rich and poor, slave and free, church and state, believer and infidel, God and greed, ship and shore, land and sea. The New Amsterdam community has often been portrayed as a mass of drinking, cursing, whoring, Sabbath-breaking roughnecks, but that reading is a misunderstanding of the subtle and not-so-subtle class distinctions that actually existed and as a deconstruction of this engraving reveals.[1]

In the man and woman in the foreground, we can feel the presence of the Reformed Church, which is seen in the background within the fort, for a well-dressed couple such as this would no doubt have been members of it, would have married in it and had their children baptized and catechized in it, and would have worshipped in it in the Dutch language. Dutch was the official language of the courts and the governing council and the only language spoken from the Dutch Reformed pulpits in New York City until 1764, 136 years after the Church's organization in 1628. (Stuyvesant in about 1650 did ask the Company to send a minister able to preach in English as well as Dutch in order to accommodate the growing numbers of English settlers on Long Island.) In the countryside, Dutch remained the language of the pulpit throughout the eighteenth century and into the nineteenth.[2]

But the engraving hides as much as it reveals, for only a small number of New Amsterdam's inhabitants was as prosperous as this couple. Prominently positioned in the foreground, the pair depicts a merchant and his wife surrounded by the bounty of the land. He stretches out his right hand, as if to say, "Look at what we have here in this land of milk and honey, this balmy temperate land where palm trees flourish, this happy land where man and wife may freely operate in the economy, where hard labor is done by slaves, where ships come and go with opportunities for riches, where church and state ensure our spiritual and civil well-being." The wife holds a brimming basket of produce, while slaves bring more produce up from the fields for her to consume at her table, or sell, as she wishes.

Bolts of fabric imported from the Netherlands recently offloaded from a ship like one of those in the harbor will be sold to the colony's inhabitants of European and African origins, and traded to the Native Americans, invisible in the picture, but present in the cargo of pelts that would have been loaded into the same ships for sale in Europe. In a bit of artistic license, indicating that the artist had surely never visited Manhattan, sugar-processing sheds shaded by palm trees enliven the middle ground, a reference both to the southern trade in rum and sugar and to New Amsterdam's role in the slave trade. But half-naked slaves are juxtaposed next to the over-dressed couple, succinctly capturing the social inequities in that pleasant land of milk and honey. As it does in many ways, the engraving, which was probably produced as a spur to emigration, glosses over the real facts of life in New Amsterdam, where few people were rich, some were comfortably well off, many were quite poor and struggling, though hard working, and a significant number were impoverished and dependent on alms from the Church.

Behind the figure of the man is a huge cask of the type used

**10.1 "Castello Plan," 1660
(redraft, 1916).**

*Collections of the New-York Historical
Society, 57812.*

to transport tobacco, which was a cash crop on Manhattan in those days. Both peltry and tobacco are bound for the Old World on one of the sailing vessels at anchor in the harbor, in exchange for the trade goods lacking in the New World, making profits on both sides of the ocean and each time they changed hands via middlemen. In addition to the transatlantic shipping that arrived in the harbor between April and October each year, trading ships from the English colonies plied the coastal waters and put into New Amsterdam harbor to conduct their business, while innumerable smaller craft on which the locals went about their business added to the bustle. Profits from trade allowed some of the more prosperous colonists to acquire from Europe not only necessary items but coveted luxury items as well.

Grandees

The few inventories that have survived from the Dutch period indicate that the prosperous minority or upper class invested in gold and silver jewelry and in household items such as silver goblets. Pearls are mentioned. Cornelis van Vorst managed the short-lived patroonship of Pavonia (Jersey City) and then stayed to accrue what was described as one of the largest private estates in New Netherland. His widow died in 1641 possessed of much cash and wampum, nineteen cambric caps, linen and lace handkerchiefs, a damask furred jacket, a cap trimmed with beaver, silver spoons, goblets, and brandy cups, jewelry, cattle, household goods, and furs.[3]

Jeremias van Rensselaer's published correspondence mentions expensive clothing sent to him from home by his mother, including a leather doublet, a Turkish grosgrain suit, a colored satin doublet, and cloth breeches. At another time, his mother, Anna, sent him a black camel's-hair hat with ribbon, English silk stockings dyed black, "shoe bows made of your ribbon," a marbled hat box, and a pair of perfumed gloves with lilies.[4] She sent a barrel "containing a bed for you [she means the bedding for a bed], a pair of understockings, six pairs of shoes, in which your name is written, and a gray hat."

His mother also sent him some goods for trading purposes. "It seems to me," she wrote to him, "that the finest wares of silk, gold or silver that one can put in a chest would be most profitable." (A quick search of the online *Correspondence* reveals thirty-nine mentions of silver items, fourteen of gold items, and twenty-one of silk items.)

The 1670 inventory of Anna's townhouse in Amsterdam, where Jeremias and his siblings had grown up, runs to eighteen pages of small type and lists many luxurious items, some of which no doubt found their way to the households of her children in New Netherland.[5] In fact, from archaeological evidence it is known that houses in New Netherland were decorated in a style that would have "fit right in at home in the Republic," in the words of two archaeologists who study it. Fragments of Dutch tiles, windowpanes decorated with enamel paint, fragile glasses, majolica plates, and home furnishings fashionable in Germany, Spain, Italy, and China have been found in New Netherland sites and indicate in the words of archaeologist Paul Huey that the colony was "no mere frontier outpost," but exhibited material culture "almost fully as sophisticated as that of the village and farms of true mid-17th century Netherlands."[6]

Later in the century, and slightly beyond the period of New Netherland, the inventory of Margrieta van Varick, a shop keeper in Brooklyn and the widow of a Reformed dominie, lists a spectacular array of objects, jewelry, clothing, and household furnishings ranging from exotic items brought from her time in the Dutch East Indies to the silk petticoats she bequeathed to her daughters.[7]

As they did in the Netherlands and were documented to do in colonial New York, wealthy families intermarried with each other and conserved and expanded their wealth by doing so. Much of their wealth was in human terms, and wills and other literary evidence suggest that children from this milieu, when they came of age, were given a slave playmate, who developed into a lifelong servant as time went on and even in some cases in adulthood the foreman of his master's farm. European men from this stratum of society were the pillars of the community, serving as deacons and elders in the church and officers in the militia and the most competent among them as member of courts and council. What about the middling sort?

The Middling Sort

For them, we turn to the Castello Plan, dated 1660, a survey of the little city made at the request of the WIC authorities in Amsterdam to inform them as to what was going on in the colony.[8] On it are about 300 houses, almost all with their own gardens and small orchards. The key to the Plan identifies a hospital, a cemetery, a ferry house, a Latin school, breweries, taverns, trading offices, a poor house, shops, warehouses, and houses for the Company's slaves. (As mentioned earlier, a number of slaves had been given their freedom in the 1640s and owned their own farms near Peter Stuyvesant's *bouwerie* in the so-called Out Ward, the area north of the wall that gave Wall Street its name.)

The key also identifies the house owners or renters in the year 1660 and their occupations, which range from accountants and attorneys right through the alphabet to bakers, brewers, carpenters, chimney sweeps, doctors, merchants, millers, a poet, many tapsters, a trumpeter, and more—every occupation in short to answer the needs and wants of a busy community. Although there are plenty of taverns, about one for every twenty households, the Castello Plan, with its attention to occupations, belies the portrait of New Amsterdam as a place of "games, drunkenness, dancing, card-playing, backgammon, tennis, ball-playing, bowling, nine pins, and racing with boats, car or wagons."

Indeed, the Castello Plan gives the impression, from their many and varied occupations, that the people of New Amsterdam were not the thieving, drunken, profane, whoring, Sabbath-breaking ne'er do wells they have often been portrayed, but hard-working, law-abiding men and women whose activities earning a living were not likely to land them in court on morals charges. We read of plenty of lawbreakers and scalawags in the New Amsterdam court records and also those from Fort Orange, but not so much of the mass of the peaceable, civic-minded, church-going folk who were too busy surviving and getting on in the world to spend their days and nights in debauchery.

In short, New Netherland was not the Wild West of the seventeenth century. There are many residents of whom almost nothing is known—the ones leading honest and boring lives that did not land them in court, and who to boot served the community as dog catchers and fence minders and on the fire brigade and the rattle watch. Further, it is documented that it was quite normal in New Amsterdam for citizens to feather their nests from as many as three occupations, from dabbling in real estate on the side, and from farming their land—as well as from the incomes their wives were able to bring in through various efforts.

Street Scenes

Contemporary images of the ordinary people of New Amsterdam do not exist. For likenesses, we have to go to the Netherlands, and since much that characterizes New Netherland originated in the fatherland, it is perfectly logical to do so. *Street Scenes: Leonard Bramer's Drawings of 17th-Century*

Dutch Daily Life, the catalog for a 1991 exhibit at Hofstra University, pictures dozens of ordinary people going about their business.[9]

The schoolmaster is one. Schools were not age segregated. All ages attended together in one room at one time. Bramer's schoolmaster grills a rather tall and mature-looking student, while other smaller, younger students gaze on, perhaps waiting for the exciting moment when the teacher will swat the big boy with the birch rods he menacingly holds in his right hand.

Literacy in the Netherlands was high in the seventeenth century, and both boys and girls attended school, as they did in New Amsterdam. At first, here, students were taught to read and write by the *voorleser*, a church official whose duties included conducting the Sabbath services, visiting the sick, consoling mourners, and catechizing the children using the Heidelberg Catechism, a process by which they learned church doctrine along with the alphabet. At the beginning, students would have gone for their lessons to his rooms in the building that served as a church. In 1638, a proper schoolmaster was appointed by the council, and in 1647, soon after his arrival, Peter Stuyvesant ordered a real school to be built.

On the Castello Plan, a Latin school is identified in Block B. In the Netherlands, Latin schools prepared young men for university. On Long Island, a contract between a schoolmaster and the consistory of the Reformed Dutch Church in Flatbush called for him to teach from November to May from 8 to 11 in the morning and from 1 to 4 in the afternoon. Each session was to open and close with specified prayers. A schoolmaster on the Delaware wrote in August 1657 that, "as soon as winter begins and they can no longer work the soil, old and young come to school to learn to read write and cipher." This schoolmaster received from the children's parents 30 *stivers* for each student, above his small annual salary, which was paid by the Company. He taught the alphabet, prayers, questions about the Bible, and the Catechism. He charged 60 *stivers* for older children and taught them the Lord's Prayer, the Ten Commandments, and the Apostles' Creed.

A carpenter in his shop, with his assistant in the background, was a familiar figure in New Amsterdam. In the wilderness of Manhattan Island, where every house, barn, and shed had to be built from scratch, carpenters were in high demand. As the population grew, so did demand for carpenters, masons, bricklayers, glaziers, and thatchers or roofers. From the contracts for dwelling houses and housebarns that

10.2 *"School-meester"* (School-master) from Leonaert Bramer, *Street Scenes.*
Leiden University Library, PK 3605 037

survive—nineteen from New Amsterdam—we are able to know with some certainty what the buildings looked like. Dimensions, framing details, structural bents, windows and doors, partitions, built-in beds, stairs, and exterior and interior finishes were carefully spelled out in these contracts, as they were for guard houses, bake houses, goat houses, churches, stables, sheds, barns, and various outbuildings.[10]

In another image from *Street Scenes*, bricklayers cooperate in building a house. The window frame is set in place. In the beginning, most bricks in New Amsterdam buildings came from New Haven, but by the 1650s several brickyards are known near Fort Orange, and records indicate that tons of Fort Orange bricks were shipped to New Castle on the Delaware in the 1650s, perhaps as ballast.[11]

Manufacturing bricks was an arduous process. Clay deposits had to be shoveled out of the banks of streams and left to cure in the open air. When tempered, the clay was kneaded by hand, or animals were led back and forth over it so that they kneaded it with their hooves. Then with rake and shovel, the brickmaker mixed the clay with sand and water and tamped it into frames with brick-shaped sections. When formed, he pressed the bricks out of the frames and left them to dry in a protected area, out of the rain. When the bricks were dry, he stacked them to produce a sort of kiln, with a hot wood fire in the middle, and baked them in this manner until they were done, feeding the fire all the while. Many turned out to be noggins, pluggins, and clinkers, broken and useless. It was discouraging work requiring much patience and little skill.

Wheelwrights, an occupation requiring high skill, were always in demand in New Amsterdam, but until the population began to grow rapidly in the late 1650s, there was basically only one wheelwright in the little city, Cosyn Gerritsen van Putten. He was a busy man, for everyone needed wheels—whether for dung carts, wheelbarrows, pushcarts, or wagons. Keeping wheeled vehicles in repair was a vital subcategory of this trade.[12]

Cosyn's career illustrates the ways ambitious settlers, bent on rising in the world, supplemented their incomes from their occupations by dabbling in real estate. In 1637, he received a grant for about sixty-eight acres of land in the area between today's Astor Place and Washington Square. His *bouwerie* is No. 41 on the Manatus Map. His grant for the sixty-eight acres included also a lot for a house and garden on today's Broadway. He sold the Broadway property and then acquired three other building lots on Broadway, and in 1661 a five-acre parcel of land with a house on it adjacent to Petrus Stuyvesant's *bouwerie* in the Out Ward. By this time, his business had grown, and his daughter had conveniently married a recently emigrated wheelwright from Hoorn to accommodate the demands on her aging father's business. This is a good example of how artisans and tradesmen followed the same marrying pattern as their betters: they chose spouses who could augment and conserve the family's resources. But attraction and affection for each other were also an important part of the equation. Historian Adriana van Zwieten has written that, "It was considered unseemly for parents to force undesirable partners on their offspring simply for business motives."[13]

Judging by their numbers in the population at around the time of the English takeover, the service trades (tavern-keepers, bakers, brewers, butchers, farmers, and millers) and wood, metal, and stone workers, together formed 38 percent of the total, "merchants, small traders, and professionals" (surgeons, ministers, lawyers, schoolmasters, clerks, Company officials), 30 percent, followed by the maritime trades, 11 percent, cloth and leather workers, 10 percent, and laborers 8 percent.[14]

At the very bottom of the economic ladder were slaves, who were not taxed even though they had a small income. By law they received wages for their work and were allowed to sell eggs or produce they raised or game they hunted. Some sold the fluff from the cattails that grew in swampland, used by poor people for stuffing mattresses. As skilled labor became more and more needed in the growing city, male slaves learned trades and were able to improve their economic standing.

A sizable number of settlers lacked the skills for anything but the meanest types of labor, but surviving inventories and court records indicate that those with skills came to the colony prepared with their tools and their pattern books to go straight to work, and there was plenty of work for them to do.

Women at Work

What about women's work? One secure job for a woman in New Amsterdam, although very few were needed for it, was midwife. Midwife Tryntie Jonas was an employee of the West India Company and in addition to her salary received a house, the house a perk to entice a candidate for this vital position. A few wealthy women engaged in commerce in a relatively large way. Margaret Hardenbroeck, wife of Frederick Philipse, was one. But average New Amsterdam women traditionally found employment as maidservants, wet nurses,

10.3 *"Wafelverkoopster"* (Waffleseller) from
Leonaert Bramer, *Street Scenes.*
Leiden University Library, PK 3605 020.

10.4 *"Visverkoopster"* (Fish Wife)
from Leonaert Bramer, *Street Scenes.*
Leiden University Library, PK 3605 015.

needleworkers, sellers of second-hand clothing, laundresses, waitresses, scullery maids, tobacco twisters, and so on.

A drawing from *Street Scenes* called "Hot Warm Waffles" shows a woman carrying a tray of waffles for sale. This is the seventeenth-century version of the ubiquitous Sabrett truck, a convenience for hungry New York City passersby in a hurry and a way to eke out a living by the most unskilled members of the population, usually female. A boy in the background is consuming a waffle, and an old woman under a shedlike structure cooks more waffles over an open fire. *Street Scenes* portrays women selling milk from buckets suspended over their shoulders from a wooden yoke, and selling vegetables, cinnamon cakes, nuts, barrels of butter, old clothes, stoneware, and mustard, scooped at her door from the mustard seller's pot into the customer's waiting mustard bowl.

Fishwife was another occupation taken up by women. According to Donna Barnes, "fishwives, and other market women, were known to be vigorous defenders of what they took to be their rights and prerogatives." Some were exceedingly sharp-tongued, she goes on: "Fights between them while not common, were not unusual. Competition between them was often keen as they tried to sell fish to customers. A fishwife might denigrate her competitor's wares while extolling the freshness and succulence of her own." In the archipelago that was New Amsterdam, fishwives had an abundant supply of product to hawk and a raft of competitors. In her tactics for beating out that competition, she has come down to us, in Webster's definition, with the reputation of a "scurrilously abusive woman." (Thus the expression: "screaming like a fishwife.")

Women in the Law

Why might fishwives and other market women have become abusive? Barnes's allusion to women's rights and prerogatives is telling. Women were jealous of and protective of their standing in the law, which guaranteed them the right to participate in the economy. The legal rights of a woman of Dutch background defined her status in the community, permitted her to buy and sell in the economy, and considered her a partner to her husband in their marriage. She could own property jointly with him, and she was responsible with him for their debts. She could make contracts, and she could sue and be sued. Under Roman-Dutch law, her husband was the legal administrator of their joint estate, and he could dispose of her portion of their property without her consent. If he did this, or if he mismanaged their affairs, she had the legal ability to take him to court. But one study of women in the Albany area found that this did not happen.[15] The companionate character of marriage in Dutch culture was conducive to cooperation, mutual trust, and general cordiality, rather than suspicion and confrontation.

Married Folk

The court records of New Amsterdam reinforce the idea that marriage was regarded as a partnership of two companionable people in a relationship that had the economic structure of a joint venture. When men and women appear in court in an adversarial position, almost none of the cases involve husbands and wives. Yet in one study of 100 cases of slander and debt, men slandered women three times more than women slandered men, and women sued men for payment or satisfaction of a contract almost four times more than men sued women.[16]

The male/female slander charges suggest that, in the fragile New Amsterdam economy, men benefited by casting doubt on women's character and thus on their reliability in fulfilling contracts, and the debt cases suggest that men resented women's power in the market place and the special benefits the law provided for women: men could be sued for the whole of their debts, but women for only half, and the law even allowed a wife to renounce her interest in the marital estate and thus not be held responsible for any debts against it. This could make a man mad.

In another study of 957 cases in which New Amsterdam women and men went to court to settle business or property disagreements, or accusations of slander, an economy in which every *stiver* counted may have been a causative factor. A woman's ability to participate in the economy was a plus to her husband and an important factor in the family's economic progress. But her special protections in the law could have represented for other men unfair competition for a share of a finite market, and such resentments may explain the numbers of times men took other men's wives to court.[17]

The Poor

Those who fell through the cracks and ended up at the bottom of the economic ladder were often there through the vicissitudes of fate: failing health, the death of a spouse or of parents, old age. For the relief of their needs, the government adopted various strategies. It stipulated that a portion of fines levied against miscreants be assigned to support the poor; it relieved the poor and infirm of certain fees and taxes; and it established an

110

Orphan Masters' Court to oversee the care of children left without parents.

These measures being insufficient to cover the need, it established poor houses, both in New Amsterdam and in Beverwijck. Until recently, historians believed that the first poor house in the colonies appeared in Boston in 1664, but Janny Venema has found proof of a poor house in Beverwijck twelve years before this, in 1652, at a time when the population of this burgeoning community was approaching that of Manhattan's.[18]

In what were effectively America's first "banks," in both New Amsterdam and Beverwijck, the Reformed Dutch Church stepped in with its deacons' funds, which were supplied largely by congregational contributions. The deacons kept careful records both of income from congregational giving to plate and poor box and income from interest on money loaned, as well as records of what they meted out to the needy. Again, church and state worked hand in hand to address an ever-present problem in all communities: that "the poor ye shall always have with you."

Venema translated a 250-page volume of the account books of the Dutch Reformed Church in Beverwijck that reveals a wealth of information about life in the colony.[19] For instance, the court under Petrus Stuyvesant patented a lot to the deacons for a garden for the poor, where the poor would be the gardeners. The deacons paid the poor to string sewant, or wampum. The poor were given "small beer," a drink purposely made weak by repeated sievings. The deacons paid women to make shirts and chemises and other garments for the needy. They supplied shoes and stockings for those without. They housed lunatics with willing families. An Indian stole money from the deacons' fund while the deacons were counting the sewant. The deacons paid women for wet-nursing infants, supplied cloth for diapers. They also supplied the pall, the cloth to cover the coffin, for eighteen children in the years 1654 and 1655 alone. Dry numbers put a human face on a frontier community in seventeenth-century New York and reveal the human tragedies and human charity that attempted to deal with them.

Africans

In the crowd at the fort on the day of the peace treaty to end Kieft's War (Chapter Five) were no doubt some with mixed feelings about Kieft, because he was not the complete villain that history has portrayed him. In fact, some in the crowd may have been quite grateful to him. These were the slaves who had petitioned for their freedom in 1640 and to whom he had given not only their freedom but title to the land on which they and their families lived and farmed. As one historian has pointed out, the formal granting of land to them "conferred not only a symbol of independence, but also of social stature and a degree of financial security. In an age before banking, one of the sharpest divisions in society was between landed and landless persons. Landowners were responsible people who supported the community and government through property taxes. And landholding was virtually a prerequisite for a young man to seek a wife."[20]

The freedmen of New Amsterdam did seek wives. At least twenty-six black couples married in the New York Dutch Reformed Church between 1639, when the records survive, to 1664, and probably quite a few more. The baptisms of sixty-one black children are recorded between 1639 and 1655, when the practice was curtailed. That the baptismal witnesses were very often Dutch neighbors of the freedmen and their wives suggests their involvement in each other's lives beyond mere geographical proximity.

The Africans who appear in New Netherland, however, were different from everyone else. They were involuntary emigrants, unlike their European counterparts, who came of their own volition, and stayed or left of their own volition, as they wished. The African had no opportunity to say no to his forced entry, and no legal opportunity to leave. Yet, the lives of Africans and Europeans were inescapably linked, as the former served the latter, as they worked side by side in the fields, as they shared a common roof, as they helped each other in childbirth and in sickness and in death, as they were exposed to each other's customs and traditions, as the latter witnessed to the baptisms of slave infants, as slave and free children played together, as their parents mingled in church and court and street and grappled with the everyday problems of survival.

In 1978, Joyce D. Goodfriend described the beginnings and the evolution of the institution in New Amsterdam, from the first Africans acquired as bounty from Spanish prizes captured on the high seas in the 1620s to the entrenchment of a slave-trading network open to private entrepreneurs by 1660. Recently she has suggested that the immigration history of New Netherland be reapproached to incorporate Africans into it on an equal basis with Europeans in order to "appreciate the common humanity" of both strands of immigration, and to heighten our perception of how the experiences of the two were similar and how they differed.[21]

Who Were "They"?

This brief discussion of the people of New Netherland tells us that they

112

fell into different social classes and a little of what they did when they got here, but who were "they"?

Only half of them were Dutch, as historian David Steven Cohen discovered from a demographic analysis.[22] The rest were French, German, English, Scandinavian, and so on. They were Calvinists, Lutherans, Catholics, Jews, Mennonites, Quakers, and even a Muslim. The Africans and Indians among them worshiped gods of their own understandings.

Many of them, having sought religious toleration in the Netherlands before emigrating again across the Atlantic, formed another melting pot in New Netherland, where they tolerated each other's cultural differences, bowed to court and council, the strong centralized and authoritarian government whose word was law, went about making their way as best they could, played and partied, drank and caroused, worked hard, served their communities. Some prospered. Some stoically endured. Some faded away leaving barely a trace of their presence.

And Why Did They Come?

When asked why he had climbed Mt. Everest, English mountaineer George Mallory famously said, "because it's there." And that is one reason prospective colonists came to New Netherland: because it was there.

They came, as immigrants always do, for adventure, a change of scene, a look-see, to avoid a sticky situation at home, but mostly they came, especially starting in the 1650s, with a hope for economic betterment. The late 1640s and the early 1650s in New Netherland, when peace with the Indians was achieved (for a time), when Brazil, taken over by the Portuguese, was no longer an option, when New Sweden was dissolved, and when the boundary problems with the English were settled, at least in Connecticut, coincided with a period of economic down turn in the Netherlands resulting in unemployment, and this motivated some to come to find work and a brighter future than seemed in store for them at home.

They went back and forth across the ocean with amazing frequency, to give birth, to hire workers as their businesses expanded, to go before the authorities seeking redress for their injustices, to see family and "the friends," as they called them, and to collect legacies. For them the Atlantic was a pond, as it is today, although one it took longer to cross, and they made of their Atlantic world a brave mixture of Dutch traditions and customs on the one hand and innovations necessitated by the novel features of frontier America in the seventeenth century on the other.

11
THE LEGACY

For a colony that lasted for only about four decades, or five, if the Restitution period in 1673-1674 is counted, New Netherland left a large imprint. We can find its legacy today in the many Dutch words in our language, in foods such as doughnuts and coleslaw (*oly-koecks* and *koolsla*), in our religious history, in the material culture of New York and New Jersey and beyond, in our founding political ideas, and in the question of Dutchness itself.

What and Who Are Dutch?
Starting with the question of Dutchness, we recall that in New Netherland only about half of the population was actually from the Dutch Republic and among that half many had emigrated from provinces within the Republic that each had its own distinctive culture. The colony was a babble of voices representing numerous places not only in the United Provinces but all over Europe, the British Isles, and Africa, as well as the sounds of the many Indian languages that were spoken.[1]

The definition of "Dutch" is complicated by the fact that in the Netherlands itself in the seventeenth century the population was only about half Dutch. Estimates are that of the total population of two million, about half a million were permanent immigrants who had come to the thriving and tolerant Republic from other parts of Europe for economic, religious, or political reasons. Transient migrants employed in the Dutch army, the merchant fleets, and migrant seasonal labor vastly increased this number. Some of these persons learned to speak Dutch, married Dutch persons, and affiliated themselves with the Reformed Dutch Church. And some of them subsequently emigrated to New

Netherland, where although they were culturally Dutch by this time, they also continued to remember their own original cultural norms, mores, customs, and patterns of thought and behavior, contributing to the increasingly colorful social mix.

Another complicating factor in defining what is or is not Dutch is that some of the inhabitants of New Netherland had no history at all of a sojourn in the Netherlands and thus no firsthand acquaintance with Dutch culture and customs. Yet in the New World, they chose to identify themselves with Dutch customs, language, religion, and philosophical outlook. Their reasons were probably rooted in the appeal of characteristics that they perceived as associated with the Dutch Republic, at least in relation to other places: inclusivity, tolerance, the value placed on civic concord, pragmatism, charity, humanism, liberty, literacy, the relatively enlightened Dutch attitude toward women, the merits of Dutch law over English, and the inescapable fact that the ruling elite in New Netherland was largely Dutch.

Their mindset persisted and was handed down over the generations. They were Dutch, whether they were or not. As historians Willem Frijhoff and Jaap Jacobs recently put it, "The historical awareness of being descendants of the founders of the new state, regardless of their origin or race, and being the distant representatives of the national tradition of the Dutch, were the longest [manifestations of Dutch culture] to endure."[2] As late as 1858, the weekly newspaper of the Reformed Dutch Church could say this: "So many of the best Yankees of New-England are becoming Dutchmen . . . that we seem to be progressing backwards toward the time when the Pilgrim Fathers forsook the bondage of their own country for a home, and freedom, and peace in Holland."[3]

And seven years before the beginning of the twentieth century, a Reformed Dutch minister could say this: "As a person of ancestry largely Dutch, I am proud to take my Dutch blood to a Dutch church every Sunday, and as a minister of Christ I am proud to stand in this pulpit and preach the same doctrines and use the same sacramental forms that have been used on the soil of New York since New Amsterdam was a trading post." The irony is that his middle name, Du Bois, suggests a French ancestry.[4]

Because the Dutch pretty much stayed put for generations on the farms and large tracts of land their ancestors had secured in the seventeenth and eighteenth centuries, the Reformed Church played a

11.1 La Roe Van Horn House, Mahwah, NJ, c. 1750.
Mahwah Museum Society, Inc.

part in the lively social life of New York and New Jersey. From Albany down the Hudson Valley into the Hackensack, Passaic, and Raritan valleys, Reformed Church members' intensely active social lives centered around church-related activities, often as many as six or eight a week, and a diverse range of wholly secular pastimes, shared always with the same local people. As Reformed people mingled almost exclusively with others reared in the same religious culture as themselves, shared values, beliefs, mores, expectations, and customs were constantly buttressed in the multitudinous and intertwining activities of church year and secular year. Daily face-to-face contacts by the same people with the same people allowed Dutchness daily to reinvigorate itself—and to color the way outsiders viewed the area. They viewed it as "Dutch."

Discussion of what Dutchness is and means continues and will continue. There will be no last word. But as Frijhoff and Jacobs have pointed out, after the English takeover of the colony, the original European population developed a "Dutch ethnic sensibility," and "this ethnification process led to the gradual adoption of the term *Dutch* as the name for the remaining group of colonists from the Dutch period of whatever origin."[5] This process happened more visibly in the countryside, especially in Bergen and Rockland counties and in the river valleys of New Jersey and the upper Hudson and Mohawk valleys, than in the city.

Material Legacy

In these areas of the former New Netherland, the material culture of the Dutch is everywhere evident. The best way to experience it is to tour it, using as a guide *Exploring the History of Dutch New York*, a handbook whose publication was inspired by the 400th anniversary of Henry Hudson's voyage of discovery in 1609, hereafter referred to as *Exploring*.[6]

But a caution is in order: Aside from Dutch place names and street names in phone books and on signage throughout the region, almost nothing tangible from the period of New Netherland remains to be seen. The material culture that is considered "Dutch" or Dutch Colonial or Dutch American, particularly such items in the landscape as houses, barns, and Reformed churches, dates with a few exceptions from the eighteenth into the early nineteenth centuries, with a burst of Dutch Colonial Revival style in the late nineteenth into the twentieth centuries. Artist L. F. Tantillo, trained as an architectural designer, but with a deep interest in the historical background of New Netherland, portrays in his paintings what are likely to be the closest approximations to the actual houses, barns, windmills, forts, farms, and people of the colony. A number of these are reproduced in this book. Many others can be viewed on the artist's website, www.lftantillo.com.

Exploring lists 177 sites to investigate, fifty-three in New York City, sixty-two in the Hudson Valley, fifty-four in New Jersey, and eight in Delaware. Hundreds of eighteenth-century Dutch Colonial houses, only a few of which could be included in *Exploring*, speckle the region, 200 in Bergen County, New Jersey, alone, most of them privately owned and owner-occupied. These houses historian David Steven Cohen has called Dutch American rather than Dutch Colonial, because they represent a new and distinct regional culture that developed in the century after the fall of New Netherland, a culture that in house architecture combined Dutch and English floor plans, framing, and roof styles in a new hybrid form, unique to the area.[7]

In *Exploring*, most of the eighteenth-century houses pictured and mapped are house museums open to the public, as are the few included from the seventeenth century. These offer a first-hand experience of the antiquity that survives, such as it is. To mention only one of the most obvious and ambitious, Philipsburg Manor in Sleepy Hollow, New York, is a working farm with period rooms in its manor house, a Dutch barn, and a gristmill. Docents demonstrate spinning, weaving, cooking, boat building, and the grinding of corn just as the slaves and family of Frederick Philipse carried them out in the seventeenth and eighteenth centuries.

Three museums in Manhattan have impressive collections of Dutch paintings from the Netherlands and artifacts from New Netherland: the Museum of the City of New York, the New-York Historical Society, and the Metropolitan Museum of Art, as well as the Brooklyn Museum in that borough. The last two have incorporated actual period houses and rooms in their galleries.

Upriver 150 miles north of Manhattan, Albany has many attractions for history tourism. The Albany Institute of History and Art has a replica of an early Dutch-style interior and a collection of Dutch colonial art and artifacts. Nearby, the New York State Museum devotes space to the area's Dutch past as known through archaeological finds, and several late eighteenth-century Albany mansions attest to the prosperity of the descendants of the original Van Rensselaer, Ten Broeck, and Schuyler settlers. Crailo State Historic Site, built in the early eighteenth century on the east bank of the Hudson in Rensselaer, NY, focuses solely on the Dutch settlers of the seventeenth century and their culture, the only museum in North America to do so.

The Bronck House in Coxsackie, dating from 1663, is the oldest house in the Upper Hudson Valley. The De Clark/De Wint House, 1700, is the oldest in the Lower Hudson Valley. Both are open to the public. Brooklyn boasts a number of historic houses.

Historical societies throughout the area possess and display artifacts, clothing, and decorative items dating from the Dutch period and thereafter. The Bergen County Historical Society in River Edge, New Jersey, is known for its recreations of Pinkster in May (a celebration, with frolicking and colored eggs, of the appearance of the Holy Spirit to the Apostles fifty days after the Resurrection), and the feast day of St. Nicholas in December, as well as frequent lectures on the time when the population of Bergen County was largely "Dutch." One of its treasured possessions is an Indian dug-out canoe unearthed from the muck of the Hackensack River.

The Mabee Farm on the Mohawk River in Rotterdam Junction, New York, is the oldest extant structure in the Mohawk Valley. With its new education center, it sits on the site of a fur-trading post where canny private traders met the Indians to purchase their best peltries before the Indians continued on their way to Schenectady village and its traders, none the wiser of the prior transactions. Schenectady, founded in 1661 by the relative of Kiliaen van Rensselaer and his representative in the colony Arent van Curler and fifteen Beverwijck families, was the site of a devastating attack by a combined French and Indian force in 1690. It is steeped in seventeenth- and eighteenth-century Dutch history, architecture, and culture, especially in the stockade area. The same is true of Kingston and its stockade area.

If an actual tour is not possible, take a virtual tour of New Amsterdam by visiting the website of the New Amsterdam History Center (www.newamsterdamhistory.org).

The mission of the NAHC is to encourage public exploration of the early history of New Amsterdam and New York City through a visual experience based on a broad and deep collection of documents and images. A work in progress, the 3D virtual tour of Stone Street in 1660, based on the Castello Plan and the images of artist Len Tantillo, is possible through Google Earth technology. The site is interactive and provides links to partner organizations, to the PBS video "Dutch New York," and to the New Netherland Institute's comprehensive and constantly updated bibliography.

Religious Legacy

The Reformed Dutch Church, which in an attempt to expunge its "foreign" image officially changed its name in 1867 to the Reformed Church in America, was ubiquitous in the Dutch culture area in the nineteenth century. From 181 church buildings in 1826, the number grew to 382 in 1870 and the number of families from 9,521 to 33,901, served by 425 pastors. Estimated total church membership in 1870 of 168,826 was twenty times the population of all of New Netherland in 1664.[8]

The growth of the Reformed Dutch Church was exponential after the Revolution, and by the middle of the nineteenth century, the denomination had become a major player in the ecclesiastical history of New York and New Jersey. Reformed ministers and their congregations participated with vigor in all of the missionary, evangelical, moral-reform, and benevolent societies of the day, and in the nineteenth-century age of revivals these societies were legion. The mark they made on each other and on America's civic history cannot be underestimated.

The river valleys and towns of former New Netherland today abound with Reformed churches. The First Reformed Church in Albany displays the hour-glass pulpit used by its pastor, Gideon Schaets, in 1656, when Albany was Beverwijck. The Reformed Church on the Green in Hackensack displays on the façade of the present church on the site the signature stone of its first pastor in the 1680s, Guiliam Bertholf, his initials engraved in a tulip. The Sleepy Hollow Reformed Church, organized by Bertholf in 1694, still stands as it did when he preached in it. Union College in Schenectady is associated in its origins with the Reformed denomination. Queens College in New Brunswick, New Jersey, received its charter in 1766 after energetic lobbying by Reformed ministers. In the nineteenth century Queens evolved into Rutgers University, with the New Brunswick Theological Seminary retaining today the original function of Queens of training candidates for the Reformed ministry.

Yes, Dutchness lives!

Political Legacy

After the English takeover in 1664, life went on much as it had. The Articles of Transfer that Petrus Stuyvestant was required to sign at the takeover were generous.[9] The Dutch were allowed to retain their farms and houses, arms and ammunition, goods and ships, and their taverns. They were free to come and go as they had a mind to. They could continue trading as they had. They could continue to "enjoy the liberty of their consciences in Divine Worship and church discipline." Although they had to concede that other religions were equally to be tolerated in English New York, the Dutch grew their Reformed Church slowly but surely and retained the Dutch language in the pulpit for a century, much longer in the countryside.

The Dutch could not be pressed to serve in war, or have any soldier quartered in their houses without being paid. They could continue to "enjoy their own customs concerning their inheritances," which entailed treating heirs of both sexes equally, contrary to the English system, which favored the first-born son. And strikingly, the officers and soldiers in the fort were allowed to march out with their arms, "drums beating, colors flying and matches lighted," and if any of them wished to turn to farming, fifty acres of land from the Royal Governor would be theirs.

The English made little attempt to change Dutch place names, aside from New Amsterdam to New York, and Beverwijck to Albany.

Dutch customs persisted for centuries afterward. Dutch marrying patterns, agricultural practices, games and pastimes, child-rearing customs, and especially, as the historian David William Voorhees writes, the "ingrained traditions of diversity and localism" that the Dutch had established in New Netherland, went on undisturbed.[10]

In the Dutch Republic, the provinces (or "states") were only loosely united for defensive purposes in the States General. They were independent of each other, and each province had its own autonomous governing body, laws, and political culture. Voorhees' term *diversity and localism* describes the resulting overlapping and competing jurisdictions among provinces, towns, and manorial estates, duchies, counties, and lordships. The "most noticeable legacy of the Dutch," he writes, "is in the political geography of the mid-Atlantic states."

Political geography has been defined as a branch of geography that deals with boundaries and subdivisions of nations, states, and cities. As applied to New Netherland, the takeover by the English in 1664, a political event, "was not catastrophic for most of the residents," Voorhees goes on. In other words, the political geography of New Netherland, even after it became New York, New Jersey, and parts of Connecticut, Delaware, and Pennsylvania, remained Dutch, not English, for a good long time. The municipalities and villages of the Dutch were not eradicated by the English, and the English retained the county and patroonship system of the Dutch rather than English models, simply renaming patroonships manors.

The consequence, Voorhees writes, "was a tangled web of governments, traditions, and jurisdictions [that was transmuted to New Netherland], and in New York, as in the Republic, complicated the decision-making process and resulted in intercommunal bickering that persists into the twenty-first century."

In the Dutch provinces, towns dominated the countryside, and merchant oligarchies dominated the towns, traditions the Dutch introduced to New Netherland, where two towns, Beverwijck and New Amsterdam, dominated the colony. This "political geography" survives in New York State today, with Albany, up-river, being the State Capitol, and New York the powerful down-river financial, arts, and medical center, and with a powerful Governor in Albany often at odds with a powerful Mayor in New York City.

In New Jersey the same is true. These ancient patterns of jurisdiction still afflict her citizens. Ranked forty-seventh in size among the fifty states, New Jersey has 566 municipalities, forty of which have

**11.2 Sleepy Hollow
Reformed Dutch
Church, c. 1698,
Tarrytown, NY.**

Janie Couch Allen.

fewer than 10,000 in population. Of these 566 municipalities, six are large cities of over 100,000, and sixteen are towns and small cities of 60,000 to 100,000, leaving 544 villages, townships, and boroughs of fewer than 60,000. And every town among them has its own school district and some more than one, all guarded proudly, passionately, and possessively by their autonomy-loving citizens.

Bergen County, more than any other county in the state, reflects the pattern laid down in the seventeenth century, the "political geography" resulting from the influence of Dutch traditions, with seventy-four separate school districts, all vying for federal and state aid, all possessed of a well-paid superintendent of schools, principals for each school, administrative staffs and teachers and teachers' aides for each school, and a harried support staff of librarians, nurses, guidance counselors, school psychologists, and on and on, shuttling busily among the schools. A wasteful and inefficient system, thanks to the Dutch!

Nor did the English takeover drive the Dutch out into the wilderness. Historian Joyce Goodfriend has noted that, as the eighteenth century began, a full generation after the takeover, the Dutch in New York City were a slight majority of the city's population. "Possessed of an extremely wealthy elite and a strong numerical and institutional base, the Dutch were not in danger of wholesale displacement from their traditional place in the city's social structure." They also continued strong in the city's political culture. From 1687 to 1707, the Dutch held an average of 58 percent of 545 offices from alderman to constable. The English held 29.5 percent, the French 11 percent, and Jews 1 percent. In the period from 1708 to 1730, the Dutch gained in political participation, holding 65 percent of 690 positions, again from alderman to constable, as compared to 26 percent for the British, 7 percent for the French, 1 percent for Jews, and 7 percent for Germans.[11]

Bruce M. Wilkenfeld agrees. During the years 1689 to 1733, he found that the "predominance of the leaders [on Manhattan] associated with the Dutch Reformed Church reflected the numerical superiority of that denomination within the city and continued a pattern that had prevailed since the first days of settlement." In the period 1734-1775, he found that the numerical superiority of Dutch Reformed laymen in the Common Council actually increased, and did not come to an end until after the Revolution.[12]

Our Founding Documents

The political legacy of the Dutch had other manifestations, which by

123

the nineteenth century had largely been forgotten. In 1892, however, a lawyer and self-trained historian named Douglas Campbell published *The Puritan in Holland, England, and America: An Introduction to American History*, in which he acquainted the general American public with America's Dutch connection. The public read in amazement the findings of Mr. Campbell. Among his most striking assertions, Campbell argued persuasively that the American Declaration of Independence was modeled on the Dutch declaration of independence from Hapsburg Spain, the so-called Act of Abjuration of 1581, that the U.S. Constitution bears a striking resemblance to the 1579 Union of Utrecht, the de facto Dutch Constitution, and that echoes of the 1664 Articles of Transfer are heard in the U.S. Bill of Rights.

The modern scholar James R. Tanis has written that, "The true heart of the Dutch impact on America lies in the critical political and economic forces by which The Netherlands affected the American scene. Foremost were the traditions of union and liberty, symbolized by the Union of Utrecht," which helped to shape the Articles of Confederation and the American constitutional debates of 1787.[13] As for the Declaration of Independence, its list of grievances against King George III is so similar to the Act of Abjuration's list of Dutch grievances against Spain's King Philip II that scholars ever since Campbell wrote believe that Thomas Jefferson used it as a model.[14]

Campbell's 1893 obituary noted that his book had "raised a considerable storm of comment and controversy on both sides of the Atlantic." English critics condemned it as robbing England of a "previously-acknowledged influence in the formation of certain American institutions." In Holland, on the other hand, it "was received with great enthusiasm, and the scholars at Leyden united in the assertion that the reasoning and deductions of the author were unassailable and of the highest interest."

The Dutch Consul General presented Campbell with a very special inkstand "as a tribute of appreciative esteem for his noble work." The inkstand was fashioned from the oak of a timber from a house where the Pilgrims had lived in Leiden before emigrating to America, a not-so-subtle poke with a sharp stick in England's eye. A review in *The American Law Register and Review* noted that Campbell made "short work of the popular assumption that the people of the United States are an English race, and that their institutions . . . derived from England." Rather, they are "partly Roman and partly Germanic," and have come down to us "via the Netherlands, where were preserved for many ages the Roman institutions and the Germanic ideas of freedom."[15]

A word of caution, though. Constitutional scholars since have discerned myriad sources for the Declaration of Independence and the U. S. Constitution, Greek, Roman, English, Dutch, Germanic, and French. It is important not to claim too much for any one of them but to see them as a pool of enlightened thought from which our founding documents emerged.

The Last Word

Different historians find different things to be New Netherland's main legacy. But if we probe into the subject, we can probably safely agree with David W. Voorhees that the English takeover of New Netherland was not a catastrophe for the culture of the region settled by the Dutch; it persisted. And we can agree with Joyce D. Goodfriend that the takeover did not lead to the wholesale displacement of the Dutch from their traditional place in the city's social structure; they persisted. Perhaps we can even agree with Evan Haefeli, who has suggested that the greatest Dutch contribution was to the growth of American pluralism, in that New Netherland succeeded in keeping the Mid-Atlantic region out of English hands until 1664. "We can thank the Dutch for the possibility that there could be New York—as well as New Jersey and Pennsylvania," he writes, for they created in the region the "unique hearth of religious and ethnic pluralism that the middle colonies became."[16]

However we account for it, the Dutch legacy to America is broad and deep and permeates and undergirds our society in ways most people scarcely imagine.

Doughnuts, anyone?

ENDNOTES

Chapter 1. The Background

1. Simon Hart, *The Prehistory of the New Netherland Company* (Amsterdam, 1959), documents the earliest years.
2. Wim Klooster, *The Dutch in the Americas* (Providence, RI, 1997), p. xvi.
3. Klooster, *Dutch in Americas*, chs. 2 and 3.
4. De Laet, quoted and translated in Klooster, *Dutch in Americas*, p. 21.

Chapter 2. The Beginnings

1. Charles W. Baird, *History of the Huguenot Emigration to America*, 2 vols. (New York, 1885), vol. 1, pp. 148-200.
2. Oliver A. Rink, *Holland on the Hudson: An Economic and Social History of Dutch New York* (Ithaca, NY, 1986), p. 76
3. Rink, *Holland on the Hudson*, p. 83
4. The original of this letter is in the National Archives in The Hague, SG, LWI, inv. No. 5751 II.
5. Nicolaes Van Wassenaer, "From the 'Historisch Verhael,'" *Narratives of New Netherland, 1609-1664*, ed. J. Franklin Jameson (New York, 1909), pp. 83, 84.
6. For a lucid discussion of the wampum industry and its introduction by the Dutch into New England, see Kevin A. McBride, "The Source and Mother of the Fur Trade: Native-Dutch Relations in Eastern New Netherland," *Enduring Traditions: The Native Peoples of New England*, ed. Laurie Weinstein (Westport, CT, and London, 1994), pp. 31-51.
7. Johannes Megapolensis, "A Short Account of the Mohawk Indians," in Jameson, ed., *Narratives*, p. 176.
8. Rink, *Holland on the Hudson*, Table 3.1, p. 89.
9. "Letter of Reverend Jonas Michaelius, 1628," in Jameson, ed., *Narratives*, pp. 117-33.
10. Megapolensis, "Mohawk Indians," in Jameson, ed., *Narratives*, pp. 163-80.
11. Simon Middleton, *From Privileges to Rights: Work and Politics in Colonial New York City* (Philadelphia, 2006), p. 231, n. 12.
12. The full title is "Privileges and Exemptions for Patroons, Masters and Private Individuals, who will Settle any Colonies and Cattle in New Netherland, resolved upon for the Service of the General West India Company in New Netherland, and for the Benefit of the Patroons, Masters and Individuals." The text in English is

printed in Jameson, ed., *Narratives*, pp. 90-96.

13. For a recent biography, see Janny Venema, *Kiliaen van Rensselaer (1586-1643): Designing a New World* (Albany, NY, Hilversum, NL, 2010).

14. Willem Frijhoff, "A Misunderstood Calvinist: The Religious Choices of Bastiaen Jansz Crol," *Journal of Early American History* 1 (2011):1-34.

15. Jaap Jacobs, "A Troubled Man: Director Wouter van Twiller and the Affairs of New Netherland in 1635," *New York History*, 85 (3):213-32. The letter: National Archives, Old West India Company, inv.nr.50, doc. 32 (20 Aug. 1635).

Chapter 3. The Kieft Years, 1638-1647

1. Willem Frijhoff, "Director Willem Kieft and His Dutch Relatives," *Revisiting New Netherland: Perspectives on Early Dutch America*, ed. Joyce D. Goodfriend (Leiden, Boston, 2005), pp. 147-204.

2. Isaac Newton Phelps Stokes, *The Iconography of Manhattan Island, 1498-1909*, 6 vols. (New York, 1915-1928), 4: 87. Vols. 1-4 are available in digital form at New York, NY: Columbia University Libraries, 2008. JPEG use copy available via the World Wide Web.

3. Van Cleaf Bachman, *Peltries or Plantations: The Economic Policies of the Dutch West India Company in New Netherland, 1633-1639* (Baltimore, 1969), p. 153.

4. Stokes, *Iconography*, 4:88.

5. James W. Bradley, *Before Albany: An Archaeology of Native-Dutch Relations in the Capital Region, 1600-1664* (Albany, NY, 2007), p. 79.

6. John A. Kouwenhoven, *The Columbia Historical Portrait of New York* (New York, 1953), pp. 35-37. The author calls attention to omissions in the key, and to a number of errors in the descriptions.

7. Stokes, *Iconography*, 4:89.

8. "Novum Belgium, by Father Isaac Jogues, 1646," in J. Franklin Jameson, ed., *Narratives of New Netherland, 1609-1664* (New York, 1909), pp. 255-63.

9. The Clarendon Papers, *Collections of the New-York Historical Society for the Year 1869* (New York, 1870), I, p. 1, and III, p. 16.

10. Jaap Jacobs, "A Troubled Man: Director Wouter van Twiller and the Affairs of New Netherland in 1635," *New York History* (Summer 2004):229-30. Quotation from letter translated by the author.

11. David Pieterze de Vries, "Short Historical and Journal-Notes," in Jameson, ed., *Narratives*, p. 202.

12. Christopher Pierce, "Resuscitating Willem Kieft: Utopian Alternatives to Dystopian Traditions," *Dreams of Paradise, Visions of Apocalypse: Utopia and Dystopia in American Culture*, ed. Jaap Verheul (Amsterdam, 2004), pp. 111-21.

Chapter 4. Kieft's War

1. Isaac Newton Phelps Stokes, *The Iconography of Manhattan Island, 1498- 1909*, 6 vols. (New York, 1915-1928),4:91.

2. The first quotation is from Jaap Jacobs, *New Netherland: A Dutch Colony in Seventeenth-Century America* (Leiden, 2005), p. 135; the second and third are from Allen W. Trelease, *Indian Affairs in Colonial New York: The Seventeenth Century* (Ithaca, NY, 1960), pp. 63, 66.

3. Paul Otto has used this nomenclature in *The Dutch-Munsee Encounter in America: The Struggle for Sovereignty in the Hudson Valley* (New York, 2006).

4. This account is based on David Pietersze de Vries, "Short Historical and Journal-Notes," J. Franklin Jameson, ed., *Narratives of New Netherland, 1609-1664*, pp. 212-16, Trelease, *Indian Affairs*, and Robert A. Grumet, *The Munsee Indians: A History* (Norman, OK, 2009).

5. Stokes, *Iconography*, 4:94, and De Vries, in Jameson, *Narratives*, ed., p. 214, n. 1.

6. De Vries, in Jameson, ed., *Narratives*, p. 216.

7. De Vries, in Jameson, ed., *Narratives*, pp. 227-28.

8. Willem Frijhoff, *Fulfilling God's Mission: The Two Worlds of Dominie Everardus Bogardus, 1607-1647* (Leiden and Boston, 2007), p. 480, n. 69.

9. "Novum Belgium, by Father Isaac Jogues, 1646," in Jameson, ed., *Narratives*, p. 260.

10. Frijhoff, *Fulfilling God's Mission*, p. 489.

11. The quoted passages are from E. B. O'Callaghan, *Documents Relative to the Colonial History of the State of New York*, 15 vols. (Albany, NY, 1853-1883), 1:210, 211.

12. O'Callaghan, *Documents Relative*, 1:211-13. *New York Historical Manuscripts Dutch*, 4 vols., trans. and ed. A. J. F. van Laer (Baltimore, 1974), 4: 279-80.

13. *Ibid.*

Chapter 5. A Feud: Director Kieft vs. Dominie Bogardus

1. Firth Haring Fabend, "'*Nieu Amsterdam*': A Copper Engraving from the Seventeenth Century," *New York History* (Summer 2004):233-46.

2. Willem Frijhoff, *Fulfilling God's Mission: The Two Worlds of Dominie Everardus Bogardus, 1607-1647* (Leiden and Boston, 2007), chs. 10-16.

3. Frijhoff, *Fulfilling God's Mission*, p. 456.

4. Isaac Newton Phelps Stokes, *Iconography of Manhattan Island, 1498- 1909*, 6 vols. (New York, 1915-1928),4:95.

5. Frijhoff, *Fulfilling God's Mission*, p. 461.

6. Frijhoff, *Fulfilling God's Mission*, p. 506.

7. Frijhoff, *Fulfilling God's Mission*, pp. 496-99.

8. Simon Groenveld, "New Light on a Drowned Princess," *de Halve Maen* (Summer 2001): 23-28.

Chapter 6. The Stuyvesant Years, 1647-1664

1. Willem Frijhoff, *Fulfilling God's Mission: The Two Worlds of Dominie Everardus Bogardus* (Leiden, Boston, 2007), p. 353.

2. "Introduction" and "The Representation of New Netherland," *Narratives of New Netherland, 1609-1664*, ed. J. Franklin Jameson (New York, 1909), p. 287.

3. Russell Shorto, *The Island at the Center of the World: The Epic Story of Dutch Manhattan & the Forgotten Colony That Shaped America* (New York, 2004), p. 171.

4. Jaap Jacobs, *New Netherland: A Dutch Colony in Seventeenth-Century America* (Leiden, Boston, 2005), p. 144.

5. Russell Shorto, *Island.*, pp. 142-43, and ch. 10. The quotation is on p. 143.

6. "The Representation of New Netherland," in Jameson, ed., *Narratives*, pp. 293-354. A drawing of the city showing its decayed condition was discovered in the Austrian

National Library in 1991. Joep de Koning has determined that the drawing was made in 1648 and was probably part of the package presented to the States General that year by Adriaen van der Donck. Joep M. de Koning, "Dating the Visscher, or Prototype, View of New Amsterdam," *de Halve Maen*, 72 (Fall 1999): 47-56.

7. Adriaen van der Donck, *A Description of New Netherland*, ed. Charles T. Gehring and William A. Starna, trans. Diederik Willem Goedhuys (Lincoln, NE, and London, 2008). The quotation is from Charles T. Gehring, trans. and ed., *Correspondence, 1647-1653* (Syracuse, NY, 2000), pp. 83-84.

8. See Edwin G. Burrows and Mike Wallace, *Gotham: A History of New York City to 1898* (New York, 1999), p. 74.

9. Martha Dickinson Shattuck, "'For the peace and welfare of the community': Maintaining a Civil Society in New Netherland," *de Halve Maen* (Summer 1999), pp. 27-32.

10. Jaap Jacobs, "'To Favor This New and Growing City of New Amsterdam with a Court of Justice.' The Relations Between Rulers and Ruled in New Amsterdam," *Amsterdam-New York: Transatlantic Relations and Urban Identities Since 1653*, ed. George Harinck and Hans Krabbendam (Amsterdam, 2005), pp. 17-29.

11. The privileges granted to the English towns on Long Island differed from those granted to Dutch villages in that certain adaptations to English custom were permitted. This shows, according to Jaap Jacobs, "that the WIC made major concessions to the English in order to populate New Netherland." *The Colony of New Netherland: A Dutch Settlement in Seventeenth-Century America* (Ithaca, NY, 2009), pp. 88-89.

12. Isaac Newton Phelps Stokes, *The Iconography of Manhattan Island, 1498-1909*, 6 vols. (New York, 1915-1928), 4:132-36.

13. Jacobs, "'To Favor This New and Growing City,'" p. 25.

14. James A. Riker, *History of Harlem Village*, rev. ed. (New York 1904).

15. Jacobs, *New Netherland: A Dutch Colony in Seventeenth-Century America*, p. 355.

16. Dennis J. Maika, "Securing the Burgher Right in New Amsterdam: The Struggle for Municipal Citizenship in the Seventeenth-Century Atlantic World," *Revisiting New Netherland*, ed. Joyce D. Goodfriend (Leiden and Boston, 2005), p. 94.

17. Simon Middleton, *From Privileges to Rights: Work and Politics in Colonial New York City* (Philadelphia, 2006), ch. 1.

Chapter 7. The Stuyvesant Years: The Fractious Fifties

1. Historian Janny Venema has given a full account of Van Slichtenhorst and his career in *Beverwijck: A Dutch Village on the American Frontier, 1652-1664* (Albany, NY, and Hilversum, NL, 1990).

2. Venema, *Beverwijck*, p. 51.

3. This topic, and how Indian lands were acquired by the Dutch, is discussed in William A. Starna, "American Indian Villages to Dutch Farms: The Settling of Settled Lands in the Hudson Valley," *Dutch New York*, ed. Roger Panetta (New York, 2009), pp. 73-90.

4. Jaap Jacobs, "The Hartford Treaty: A European Perspective on a New World Conflict," *de Halve Maen* (Winter 1995): 74-75. The quoted passage is on p. 79 and is from Edmund B. O'Callaghan and Berthold Fernow, eds. and trans., *Documents Relative to the Colonial History of the State of New York*, 15 vols. (Albany, 1853-1887), 1:486, 487. Italics added.

5. The terms of the treaty are found in *Documents Relative*, 1: 486, 487, and in

the Collected Papers of Hans Bontemantel, ed. Martha Dickinson Shattuck, www.newnetherlandinstitute.org.

6. Charles T. Gehring, "De Suyt Rivier: New Netherland's Delaware Frontier," *de Halve Maen* (Summer 1992): 21-25. For a book-length treatment, C. A. Weslager, *Dutch Explorers, Traders and Settlers in the Delaware Valley, 1609-1664* (Philadelphia, 1961).

7. Gehring, "De Suyt Rivier" (1992), p. 23; and Charles T. Gehring, "De Suyt Rivier": New Netherland's Southern Region," *de Halve Maen* (Winter, 2011):63-66. Also, Christian J. Koot, "Spanning the Peninsula: Augustine Herrman, the South River, and Anglo-Dutch Overland Trade in the Northern Chesapeake," *de Halve Maen* (Winter 2011):67-74.

8. Charles T. Gehring, ed. and trans., *Delaware Papers (Dutch Period), 1648-1664* (Baltimore, 1981), p. 29, and quoted in Gehring, "De Suyt Rivier" (1992), p. 22.

Chapter 8. The Stuyvesant Years: Wars upon Wars

1. Allen W. Trelease, *Indian Affairs in Colonial New York: The Seventeenth Century* (Ithaca, NY, 1960), p. 138.

2. In the words of William A. Starna, "American Indian Villages to Dutch Farms: The Settling of Settled Lands in the Hudson Valley," *Dutch New York: The Roots of Hudson Valley Dutch Culture*, ed. Roger Panetta (New York, 2009), pp. 74-75.

3. Trelease, "Indian Affairs, pp. 28-29; and Starna, "American Indian Villages," p. 83, where he writes that, for the Indians in the lower Hudson Valley, when furs became unavailable to them, "selling land to the Dutch was an important way these Indians were able to acquire the much-needed goods for which others traded furs."

4. James W. Bradley, *Before Albany: An Archaeology of Native-Dutch Relations in the Capital Region, 1600-1664* (Albany, NY, 2007); and Paul Otto, "Intercultural Relations between Native Americans and Europeans in New Netherland and New York," *Four Centuries of Dutch-American Relations, 1609-2009*, ed. Hans Krabbendam, Cornelis A. van Minnen, and Giles Scott-Smith (Albany, NY, and Middelburg, NL, 2009).

5. Robert A. Grumet, *The Munsee Indians: A History* (Norman, OK, 2009), pp. xxii-xxiii, p. 68.

6. José A. Brandaõ, *"Your Fyre Shall Burn No More": Iroquois Policy toward New France and Its Native Allies to 1701* (Lincoln, NE, 2007).

7. Adriaen van der Donck, *A Description of New Netherland*, ed. Charles T. Gehring and William A. Starna, trans. Diederik Willem Goedhuys (Lincoln, NE, and London, 2008), p. 74; and Starna, "American Indian Villages," pp. 74-75.

8. Oliver A. Rink, *Holland on the Hudson: An Economic and Social History of Dutch New York* (Ithaca, NY, 1986), pp. 163-64.

9. Rink, *Holland on the Hudson*, pp. 163-64.

10. Dennis Maika, "The Credit System of the Manhattan Merchants in the Seventeenth Century," *de Halve Maen* (September 1990):5-6; and Maika, "Credit, Court, and New York City Merchants in the Age of Leisler," *A Beautiful and Fruitful Place*, ed. Elisabeth Paling Funk and Martha Dickinson Shattuck (Albany, NY, 2011), pp. 37-46.

11. Rink, *Holland on the Hudson*, Figure 7-2, p. 176.

12. Rink, *Holland on the Hudson*, ch. 7 passim.

13. Simon Groenveld, "New Light on a Drowned Princess," *de Halve Maen* (Summer 2001):23-28.

Chapter 9. Church, State, and Petrus Stuyvesant

1. Some information in this chapter is from Firth Haring Fabend, "Church and State, Hand in Hand: Compassionate Calvinism in New Netherland," *de Halve Maen* (Spring 2002).
2. Constitution, Article 28, 1619, printed in Edward T. Corwin, ed., *A Digest of the Constitutional and Synodical Legislation of the Reformed Church in America* (New York, 1906), p. xxxii.
3. Arnold J.F. van Laer, ed. and trans., *Documents Relating to New Netherland, 1624-1626, in the Henry E. Huntington Library* (San Marino, Ca., 1924), pp. 2-5.
4. Berthold Fernow, ed., *Minutes of the Executive Boards of the Burgomasters of New Amsterdam* (New York, 1970), p. 115.
5. Arnold J. F. van Laer, trans., *Council Minutes, 1638-49*, New York Historical Manuscripts, 4 vols. (Baltimore, 1974), 4: 612.
6. Berthold Fernow, ed., *The Records of New Amsterdam from 1653 to 1674* , 7 vols. (New York, 1897), 7: 114.
7. Fernow, *Records*,1:48-49.
8. Van Laer, *Council Minutes*, 4:506-10.
9. Fernow, *Records*, 3:148-49.
10. Gerald F. De Jong, *The Dutch Reformed Church in the American Colonies* (Grand Rapids, MI, 1978), p. 233.
11. Fernow, *Records*, 1: 80, 109, 114.
12. Fernow, *Records*, 1:377, 113, 264, 356; Fernow, *Executive Minutes*, pp. 82, 84, 85, 88, 90.
13. Fernow, *Executive Minutes*, pp. 185-89.
14. Noah L. Gelfand, "Jews in New Netherland: An Atlantic Perspective," in *Explorers, Fortunes & Love Letters, A Window on New Netherland*, ed. Martha Dickinson Shattuck (Albany, 2009), p. 41.
15. David William Voorhees, "The 1657 Flushing Remonstrance in Historical Perspective," *de Halve Maen* (Spring 2008):11-14.
16. Henri and Barbara Van der Zee, *A Sweet and Alien Land: The Early History of New York* (London and New York, 1978), p. 354.
17. Jaap Jacobs, *The Colony of New Netherland: A Dutch Settlement in Seventeenth-Century America* (Ithaca and London, 2009) , p. 99.
18. Fernow, *Records of New Amsterdam*, 2:329-30.
19. Eric W. Sanderson, *Mannahatta: A Natural History of New York City* (New York, 2009), p. 79.

Chapter 10. The People of New Netherland

1. This image is the subject of Firth Haring Fabend, "'*Nieu Amsterdam*': A Copper Engraving from the Seventeenth Century," *New York History* (Summer 2004):233-46.
2. Rob Naborn, "Eilardus Westerlo (1738-1790): From Colonial Dominie to American Pastor" (diss. Vrije Universiteit 2011). Westerlo was pastor of the First Church of Albany (Reformed, of course).

3. Charles H. Winfield, *History of the County of Hudson, New Jersey* (New York, 1874), pp. 426-38.

4. *Correspondence of Jeremias van Rensselaer, 1651-1674*, trans and ed. A. J. F. van Laer (Albany, NY, 1932), passim.

5. Janny Venema, *Kiliaen van Rensselaer (1586-1643): Designing a New World* (Hilversum, NL, 2010), Appendix 1. The house plans of the Van Rensselaer town house at Keizersgracht 277 by Henk Zantkuijl are given in Appendix 2 of this work.

6. Anne-Marie Cantwell and Diana diZerega Wall, "Landscapes and Other Objects: Creating Dutch New Netherland," *New York History* (Fall 2008): 339, 341.

7. *Dutch New York Between East and West: The World of Margrieta van Varick*, Catalogue of Exhibit of same name, Bard Graduate Center (New York, NY, 2009-2010), ed. Deborah L. Krohn and Peter N. Miller, with Marybeth De Filippis (New York, 2009), pp. 342-64.

8. The Plan and its key are reproduced in many works, as well as on line. See Isaac Newton Phelps Stokes, *The Iconography of Manhattan Island, 1498-1909*, 6 vols. (New York, 1915-1928):2, Plate 82, and its discussion. Vols. 1-4 are available in digital form at New York, NY: Columbia University Libraries, 2008. JPEG use copy is available via the World Wide Web.

9. Donna Barnes and Jane ten Brink Goldsmith, Catalog for Exhibit *Street Scenes: Leonard Bramer's Drawings of 17th-Century Dutch Daily Life*, Hofstra University Museum (Hempstead, NY), 1991.

10. Jeroen van den Hurk, "Building a House in New Netherland: Documentary Sources for New Netherlandic Architecture, 1624-64," *From De Halve Maen to KLM: 400 Years of Dutch-American Exchange*," ed. Margriet Bruijn Lacy, Charles Gehring, Jenneke Oosterhoff (Munster, 2008), pp. 25-40.

11. L. F. Tantillo, *The Edge of New Netherland* (Albany, NY, 2011), pp. 44, 45; and personal communication from Charles T. Gehring, February 2, 2012.

12. Firth Haring Fabend, "Cosyn Gerritsen van Putten: New Amsterdam's Wheelwright," *de Halve Maen* (Summer 2007):23-30.

13. Adriana E. van Zwieten, "'[O]n her woman's troth': Tolerance, Custom and the Women of New Netherland," *de Halve Maen* (Spring 1999):3-14.

14. Joyce D. Goodfriend, *Before the Melting Pot: Society and Culture in Colonial New York City, 1664-1730* (Princeton, NJ, 1992), Table 1-1.

15. Martha Dickinson Shattuck, "Women and Trade in New Netherland," *Itinerario* 18, 2 (1994), 40-49.

16. This paragraph and the next are from Firth Haring Fabend, "Sex and the City: Relations Between Men and Women in New Netherland," *Revisiting New Netherland: Perspectives on Early Dutch America*, ed. Joyce D. Goodfriend (Leiden, Boston, 2005), pp. 279-80.

17. Linda Biemer, "Criminal Law and Women in New Amsterdam," *A Beautiful and Fruitful Place*, ed. Nancy Anne McClure Zeller (Albany, NY, 1991), pp. 73-89.

18. Janny Venema, *Beverwijck: A Dutch Village on the American Frontier, 1652-1664* (Albany, NY, 1990), p. 327.

19. Janny Venema, *Deacons' Accounts, 1652-1674, Beverwijck/Albany* (Rockport, ME, 1998).

20. Peter R. Christoph, "The Freedmen of New Amsterdam," *A Beautiful and Fruitful Place: Selected Rensselaerswijck Seminar Papers*, ed. Nancy Anne McClure Zeller (Albany, 1991), p. 159.

21. Joyce D. Goodfriend, "Burghers and Blacks: The Evolution of a Slave Society at New Amsterdam," *New York History* (April 1978):124-44; and Goodfriend, "Merging the Two Streams of Migration to New Netherland," *New York History* (Summer 2011):133-50. There is a huge and ever-growing literature on slavery. For an introduction, *The Slavery Reader*, ed. Gad Heuman and James Walvin (New York, 2003); and John Thornton, *Africa and Africans in the Making of the Atlantic World, 1400-1800*, 2d. ed. (New York, 1998).

22. David Steven Cohen, "How Dutch Were the Dutch of New Netherland?" *New York History*, 62 (1981):43-60.

Chapter 11. The Legacy

1. This discussion is taken in part from Firth Haring Fabend, *Zion on the Hudson: Dutch New York and New Jersey in the Age of Revivals* (New Brunswick and London, 2000), ch. 1.

2. Willem Frijhoff and Jaap Jacobs, "Introduction," *Four Centuries of Dutch-American Relations, 1609-2009*, ed. Hans Krabbendam, Cornelis A. Van Minnen, Giles Scott-Smith (Albany, NY, 2009), p. 32.

3. *Christian Intelligencer*, May 27, 1858.

4. Fabend, *Zion on the Hudson*, p. 1. The speaker was the Reverend Henry Du Bois Mulford of Syracuse, NY, 1893. Details in the next paragraph are from *Zion*, ch. 6.

5. Frijhoff and Jacobs, *Four Centuries*, p. 36.

6. *Exploring Historic Dutch New York: New York City, Hudson Valley, New Jersey, and Delaware*, ed. Gajus Scheltema and Heleen Westerhuijs (New York, 2011).

7. David Steven Cohen, *The Dutch-American Farm* (New York, 1992).

8. Fabend, *Zion on the Hudson*, Table 5.1, p. 86.

9. These have usually been called Articles of Capitulation, but Transfer is a more accurate translation, according to Charles T. Gehring. The reason the Articles were so generous is that, because the takeover had happened in a time of truce, it was illegal, and it was thus assumed by both sides that it could and probably would be reversed.

10. David William Voorhees, "The Dutch Legacy in America," *Dutch New York: The Roots of Hudson Valley Culture*, ed. Roger Panetta (New York, 2009), ch. 13.

11. Joyce D. Goodfriend, *Before the Melting Pot: Society and Culture in Colonial New York City* (Princeton, NJ, 1992), Table 4-12, Table 8-8.

12. Bruce M. Wilkenfeld, "The New York City Common Council, 1689-1800," *New York History* (July 1971):249-73.

13. James R. Tanis, "The Dutch-American Connection: The Impact of the Dutch Example on American Constitutional Beginnings," *A Beautiful and Fruitful Place*, ed. Nancy Anne McClure Zeller (Albany, NY, 1991), p. 353.

14. Stephen E. Lucas, "*The Plakkaat van Verlatinghe*, A Neglected Model for the American Declaration of Independence," *Connecting Cultures: The Netherlands in Five Centuries of Transatlantic Exchange*, ed. Rosemarijn Hoefte and Johanna C. Kardux (Amsterdam, 1994), pp. 187-207.

15. *New York Times*, March 8, 1893. *The American Law Register and Review*, vol. 42 (Philadelphia, 1894), p. 546.

16. Evan Hafaeli, *New Netherland and the Dutch Origins of American Religious Liberty* (Philadelphia, 2012), p. 287.

CHRONOLOGY

1555
Philip II inherits control over Low Countries

1566
Beeldenstorm, Calvinist destruction of Catholic images begins

1568
Dutch revolt against Spain begins

1579
Union of Utrecht

1581
Act of Abjuration

1588
Philip II unites crowns of Spain and Portugal. Spanish Armada defeated

1602
Dutch East India Company chartered by the States General of the United Provinces

1609
Twelve Years' Truce with Spain. Henry Hudson, in command of the Dutch East India Company ship *de Halve Maen*, explores from Delaware Bay to the upper Hudson

1614
The name New Netherland first appears in an official document.
New Netherland Company licensed by the States General for four years.
Fur-trading post Fort Nassau established on Castle Island,
present-day Port of Albany

1617
Fort Nassau washed away in flood

CR

1621
End of Twelve Years' Truce with Spain. Dutch West India Company chartered by States General

1624
Fort Orange built on higher ground on mainland to replace Fort Nassau. First colonists arrive and are dispersed in four areas. Captain Cornelis May becomes first director of New Netherland

1625
Willem Verhulst arrives as second director of New Netherland

1626
Daniel van Crieckenbeeck killed while supporting a Mahican war party against the Mohawks. Peter Minuit replaces Verhulst as director. Manhattan Island purchased and scattered settlers move to it

1629
"Freedoms and Exemptions" establish the patroonship plan of colonization

1632
Peter Minuit replaced as director by Bastiaen Jansz Crol

1633-1647
Dominie Everardus Bogardus called to the Reformed Dutch Church

1633-1638
Wouter van Twiller is director of New Netherland

1638
New Sweden is established on the Delaware by Peter Minuit in employ of Sweden

1638-1647
Willem Kieft is director of New Netherland

1639
Dutch West India Company opens fur trade to all

1643-1645
Kieft's War, also known as the First Dutch-Munsee War

1647
Petrus Stuyvesant becomes Director General.
Director Kieft and Dominie Bogardus lost at sea

1650
Hartford Treaty establishes boundary between
New Netherland and New England

1651
Stuyvesant establishes Fort Casimir on the Delaware

1652
Beverwijck chartered

1652-1654
First Anglo-Dutch War

1653
Defensive wall that becomes known as Wall Street
built to forestall invasion from New England

1654
Swedes capture Fort Casimir

1655
New Amstel chartered

1655
Stuyvesant subdues New Sweden. Peach War, or
Second Dutch-Munsee War

1658-1663
Esopus War, or Third Dutch-Munsee War

1664
In a surprise attack in peacetime English naval force takes over
New Netherland and renames it New York

1665-1667
Second Anglo-Dutch War

1672-1674
Third Anglo-Dutch War

1673
Dutch naval force recaptures New York and restores New Netherland as a
Dutch colony

1674
By Treaty of Westminster between England and the Dutch Republic,
New Netherland becomes New York again

INDEX